LEAVES OF GRASS

NOTES

including

- *Life and Background*
- *A Whitman Chronology*
- *Critical Commentaries of the Poems*
- *Critical Analysis of Whitman's Style and Themes*
- *The Quintessential American Poet*
- *Whitman's Achievement*
- *Selected Bibliography*

by
V. A. Shahane, Ph.D.
Chairman, Department of English
Osmania University
Hyderabad, India

INCORPORATED
LINCOLN, NEBRASKA 68501

Editor

Gary Carey, M.A.
University of Colorado

Consulting Editor

James L. Roberts, Ph.D.
Department of English
University of Nebraska

ISBN 0-8220-0723-1

Printed in U.S.A.

1993 Printing

Cliffs Notes, Inc. Lincoln, Nebraska

CONTENTS

Life and Background 5

A Whitman Chronology 8

Critical Commentaries

From *Inscriptions* 10
"One's-Self I Sing" 10
"As I Ponder'd in Silence" 11
"For Him I Sing" 12
"To the States" 12
"I Hear America Singing" 13
"Poets to Come" 13
"To You" 14
"Thou Reader" 14
"Song of Myself" 15

From *Children of Adam* 25
"To the Garden the World" 26
"Spontaneous Me" 27
"Ages and Ages Returning at Intervals" 28
"As Adam Early in the Morning" 29

From *Calamus* 29
"In Paths Untrodden" 30
"Scented Herbage of My Breast" 30
"Whoever You Are Holding Me Now in Hand" 31
"When I Heard at the Close of the Day" 32
"Are You the New Person Drawn Toward Me?" 33
"Not Heat Flames Up and Consumes" 33
"I Saw in Louisiana a Live-Oak Growing" 33
"Full of Life Now" 34
"Crossing Brooklyn Ferry" 34
"Song of the Broad-Axe" 39
"Pioneers! O Pioneers!" 45
"Out of the Cradle Endlessly Rocking" 46
"When I Heard the Learn'd Astronomer" 48

"Beat! Beat! Drums!" 48
"Cavalry Crossing a Ford" 49
"When Lilacs Last in the Dooryard Bloom'd" 49
"As Consequent, *Etc.*" 53
"There Was a Child Went Forth" 54
"Passage to India" 54
"The Sleepers" 59
"To a Locomotive in Winter" 64
"As the Time Draws Nigh" 64
"So Long" 65
"Queries to My Seventieth Year" 66
"America" 66
"Good-Bye My Fancy" 66

Critical Analysis

Form 67
Style 67
Themes 70

The Quintessential American Poet 74

Whitman's Achievement 74

Selected Bibliography 75

Leaves of Grass Notes

LIFE AND BACKGROUND

Walt Whitman is both a major poet and an outstanding personality in the history of American literature. He rose from obscurity to monumental fame, coming to be recognized as a national figure. His achievement is great, although it has been sometimes obscured by unfair, hostile criticism—or, conversely, by extravagant praise. He is essentially a poet, though other aspects of his achievement—as philosopher, mystic, or critic—have also been stressed.

Walt Whitman was born in West Hills, Long Island, New York on May 31, 1819. His father, Walter, was a laborer, carpenter, and house builder. His mother, Louisa, was a devout Quaker. In 1823, the family moved to Brooklyn, where Walt had his schooling (1825-30). From 1830 to 1836 he held various jobs, some of them on newspapers in Brooklyn and Manhattan. From 1836 to 1841 he was a schoolteacher in Long Island, despite the paucity of his own education. The division of Whitman's early life between town and country later enabled him to depict both environments with equal understanding and sympathy. He also traveled extensively throughout America, and so could appreciate the various regions of the land.

Between 1841 and 1851 Whitman edited various periodicals and newspapers. It was, apparently, during this period that he began to compose the poems which were later published as *Leaves of Grass*.

In 1862 Walt's brother George was wounded in the Civil War. When Whitman traveled to Virginia to visit him, he saw large numbers of the wounded in hospitals. The Civil War was a major event in Whitman's career, stirring both his imagination and his sensibility and making him a dresser of spiritual wounds as well as of physical ones as he worked as a volunteer in hospitals. Lincoln's assassination (1865) also moved Whitman deeply, and several poems bear testimony of his intense grief.

In 1865 Whitman was fired from his post in the Department of the Interior in Washington because of the alleged indecency of *Leaves of Grass*. He was hired by the Attorney General's office and remained there until 1873 when he suffered a mild paralytic stroke which left him a semi-invalid. In Whitman's last years (1888-92), he was mostly confined to his room in the house which he had bought in Camden, New Jersey. Two friends, Horace Traubel and Thomas B. Harned, attended him. He died on March 26, 1892. Thus ended the lifelong pilgrimage of the Good Gray Poet (as his contemporary, critic W. D. O'Connor, called him), an immortal in American literature.

Whitman grew into almost a legendary figure, due largely to the charm and magnetism of his personality. Contemporary critics described him as a "modern Christ." His face was called "serene, proud, cheerful, florid, grave; the features, massive and handsome, with firm blue eyes." His head was described as "magestic, large, Homeric, and set upon his strong shoulders with the grandeur of ancient sculpture." These descriptions tend to make Whitman appear almost a mythical personage. But he was very much alive.

Whitman was a being of paradoxes. His dual nature, a profound spirituality combined with an equally profound animality, puzzled even his admirers. John A. Symonds, an English writer, was puzzled by undercurrents of emotional and sexual abnormality in the *Calamus* poems and questioned Whitman on this issue. Whitman's reply (August 19, 1890) is interesting: "My life, young manhood, mid-age, times South, etc., have been jolly bodily, and doubtless open to criticism. Though unmarried I have had six children—two are dead—one living Southern grandchild—fine boy, writes to me occasionally—circumstances... have separated me from intimate relations." But no trace of any children of Whitman's has been found, and it is not unlikely that he merely invented them to stave off further questions.

Whitman was truly a representative of his age and reflected its varied crosscurrents. His poetry shows the impact of the romantic idealism which reached its zenith in the years before the Civil War and also shows something of the scientific realism which dominated the literary scene after 1865. Whitman harmonizes this romanticism and realism to achieve a true representation of the spirit of America. The growth of science and technology in his time affected Whitman deeply, and he responded positively to the idea of progress and evolution. American patriotism in the nineteenth century projected the idea of history in relation to cosmic philosophy: it was thought that change and progress form part of God's design. The historical process of America's great growth was therefore part of the divine design, and social and scientific developments were outward facets of real spiritual progress. Whitman shared in this idea of mystic evolution. *Leaves of Grass* symbolizes the fulfillment of American romanticism as well as of the sense of realistic revolt against it.

Whitman visualized the role of a poet as a seer, as a prophetic genius who could perceive and interpret his own times and also see beyond time. The ideal poet, thought Whitman, portrays the true reality of nature and comprehends and expresses his genuine self. He holds a mirror to his self and to nature; he also illuminates the meaning and significance of the universe and man's relation to it. An ideal poet, he believed, is the poet of man first, then of nature, and finally of God; these elements are united by the poet's harmonious visionary power. Though the poet is concerned primarily with the world of the spirit, he accepts science and democracy within his artistic fold, since these are the basic realities of the modern world, especially that of nineteenth-century America. Recognition of the values of science and democracy is indirectly an acknowledgement of the reality of modern life. Whitman's ideal poet is a singer of the self; he also understands the relation between self and the larger realities of the social and political world and of the spiritual universe. He intuitively comprehends the great mysteries of life—birth, death, and resurrection—and plays the part of a priest and a prophet for mankind.

Leaves of Grass, ever since its first publication in 1855, has been a puzzling collection of poems. It inspires, it enthralls, and it tantalizes—and yet, the problems it poses are numerous and varied. Whitman so completely identified himself with *Leaves* ("This is no book,/Who touches this touches a man") that critics have tried to find reflections of Whitman's own life in all the imagery and symbolism of the poems. Whitman did explore and express many aspects of his personality in *Leaves.* It was he himself who created the illusion that he and his poems were identical. Through these works, he found full expression as a poet—and as a man.

The first edition (1855) of *Leaves of Grass* consisted of ninety-five pages. The author's name did not appear, but his picture was included. By the time the second edition was published in 1856, the volume consisted of 384 pages, with a favorable review by Emerson printed on the back cover. For this edition, Whitman not only added to the text, he also altered the poems which had previously been published. The third edition appeared in 1860 and contained 124 new poems. The fourth edition, published in 1867, was called the "workshop" edition because so much revision had gone into it. It contained eight new poems. The fifth edition (1871) included the new poem "Passage to India." The sixth edition, in two volumes, appeared in 1876. The seventh edition was published in 1881 and is widely accepted as an authoritative edition today, although the eighth and ninth editions are equally important. The last, which is also called the "deathbed" edition because it was completed in the year of Whitman's death (1892), represents Whitman's final thoughts. The text used here will be that of the last, or "deathbed," edition of 1892. Only the most significant poems of each section of *Leaves of Grass* will be discussed.

A WHITMAN CHRONOLOGY

1819 Born May 31 at West Hills, Huntington Township, Long Island, New York.

1823 Family moved to Brooklyn, New York.

1825-30	Attended public school in Brooklyn.
1830-31	Office boy in lawyer's office, then doctor's; then printer's apprentice.
1832-36	Various jobs: printer's devil, handyman.
1836-41	Schoolteacher in Long Island.
1841-47	Reporter and editor for various newspapers. Editor (1846) of Brooklyn *Daily Eagle*. Published (1842) *Franklin Evans, or the Inebriate*, a tract.
1848	Discharged from the *Eagle*. Visited New Orleans (worked on New Orleans newspaper) and traveled on the Mississippi River and the Great Lakes.
1849	Editor of the Brooklyn *Freeman*, a journal.
1850-54	Part-time journalist. Carpenter and house builder in Brooklyn (with father).
1855	First edition of *Leaves of Grass* published in July. It contained twelve poems and a prose preface.
1856	Second edition of *Leaves of Grass*, containing twenty additional poems.
1860	Third edition of *Leaves of Grass*. Traveled to Boston to discuss the preparation of this edition with Emerson.
1862-63	Went to Virginia to attend brother George, who had been wounded in Civil War. Did volunteer work in government hospitals.
1863-73	Lived most of the time in Washington, D.C. Worked for the government.
1864	*Drum-Taps* published.
1867	Fourth edition of *Leaves of Grass*.
1871	Fifth edition of *Leaves of Grass*. Also published *Democratic Vistas* (a prose pamphlet).
1873	Suffered mild paralytic stroke. Moved to Camden, New Jersey. Mother died.
1876	Sixth edition of *Leaves of Grass*.
1879	Traveled to St. Louis to visit his brother Jeff.
1881	Visited Boston to prepare the seventh edition of *Leaves of Grass*, published that same year.
1882	*Specimen Days* published.
1884	Bought house in Camden, where he lived the rest of his life.
1888	*November Boughs* published.

1889	Pocket-size edition of *Leaves of Grass* published for his seventieth birthday.
1891-92	Final ("deathbed") edition of *Leaves of Grass*.
1892	Died March 26. Buried in Harleigh Cemetery, Camden.

CRITICAL COMMENTARIES

INSCRIPTIONS

The 1871 edition of *Leaves of Grass* contained nine poems classified as *Inscriptions;* the 1881 edition contained twenty-four such poems, including two long ones, "Starting from Paumanok" and "Song of Myself."

The *Inscriptions* are dedicatory poems and form a preface to the main body of *Leaves of Grass*. This group of poems does not, however, indicate any well-thought-out plan or organization — it seems, rather, an improvised prologue. The themes are diverse, the symbolism is varied, and the only thing which really holds the group together is the poet's clear intention to provide a prologue. The lack of unity in theme and the general lack of close-knit organization is partly due to Whitman's continual reclassification of his poems. Some of the poems in *Inscriptions* were at first included with other sections of *Leaves*.

The arrangement of the poems in *Inscriptions* does, however, suggest the general arrangement of *Leaves of Grass*, a natural biographical sequence in which the early poems deal with youth and the later ones with old age and approaching death.

"One's-Self I Sing"

Although the poet sings of the self as "a simple separate person," he also sees it as part of "the word Democratic," which represents the mass of people. He sings of "the Form complete," the female as well as the male, of "Life immense in passion, pulse, and power," and the "Modern Man."

This small (nine-line) poem is really a preface to all the others in *Leaves of Grass*. Whitman says he will sing of all physiology (the branch of biology dealing with the functions and processes of living organisms), for neither the physiognomy (outward appearance) nor the brain is worthy of being celebrated independently. He lists the subjects and themes he will deal with: "One's-self" (the unit of self or individuality), "physiology . . . the Form complete" (the kinship of the body and the spirit which he will emphasize throughout *Leaves*), and "Life"—in short, the "Modern Man," who, according to Whitman, is conscious of "self" but at the same time is aware of being part of the large mass of democracy.

"As I Ponder'd in Silence"

As the poet meditated on his poetry, a phantom, beautiful but terrible, the muse of ancient poets, appeared before him. The spirit asked him about the themes of his poetry and asserted that it is "the theme of War, the fortune of battles,/The making of perfect soldiers," which are the proper themes for poets. Whitman proudly answered that he, too, dealt with war and victory. But in Whitman's universe, war is waged for "life and death, for the Body and for the eternal Soul." And so he, too, promotes the cause of "brave soldiers."

Whitman here attempts to establish a correlation between his poetry and traditional poetry. The subjects of Whitman's poetry are not the established themes of traditional poetry, specifically the epic. An epic is a long narrative poem about the deeds of a historical, traditional, or legendary hero, with a background of warfare or the supernatural, written in a highly dignified style and following other formal conventions of structure. Whitman's answer to the muse's query makes clear his position. He feels that his poems do satisfy the criteria of the epic, for they deal with the basic and universal problems of man. An epic reflects the main quality of an age, and in this sense Whitman's

Leaves of Grass is an epic poem. Traditional epics deal with war and heroism; Whitman writes about them, but Whitman's wars are eternal and his battlefield is life; the "soldiers" are all of humanity, and their victory is the triumph of the spirit over matter.

"For Him I Sing"

The "him" for whom the poet sings is his ideal man of imagination and vision. "I raise the present on the past," Whitman says, comparing this process to the growth of a tree from its roots. He also depicts, he says, the ideal man's movement in space and in time. He is a "law unto himself."

This poem is cryptic and vague. "Him" is an ambivalent pronoun – no antecedent noun is stated for it. We must infer for whom the poet sings. The person for whom Whitman has greatest admiration is the embodiment of his ideal of personality. He is the thinking man, the man of vision. Whitman believes that the poet is able to unite the past with the present. Past and present are inseparable because they are part of the flow of time. Poetry, like a tree, grows organically and inwardly. The growth of personality is also organic and unified.

This short poem has a symbolic quality, though the poetic utterance is oblique and cryptic. The poet's function in uniting past and present is one of the basic ideas of Whitman's concept of poetry.

"To the States"

The poet calls upon the cities and the states to "*resist much, obey little.*" Unquestioning obedience will lead to slavery, and if a nation is enslaved, it may never regain its freedom.

This is one of the small, though significant, dedicatory poems in *Inscriptions*. Whitman feels that one of the essential features of a free, democratic society is its diversity of opinions. Blind obedience must be resisted, or the state risks losing all its

freedom. Implicit in the concept of obedience is t
totalitarianism. The poem suggests the democr
Whitman's poetic cosmos. The concept of democı
the significant themes of *Leaves of Grass*.

"I Hear America Singing"

The poet hears the "varied carols" of all the people who contribute to the life and culture of America. The mechanic, the carpenter, the mason, the boatman, the shoemaker, and the woodcutter all join in the chorus of the nation. The singing of the mother, the wife, and the girl at work expresses their joy and their feeling of fruition. These are highly individualistic men and women. Each person sings "what belongs to him or her and to none else."

This poem underscores Whitman's basic attitude toward America, which is part of his ideal of human life. The American nation has based its faith on the creativeness of labor, which Whitman glorifies in this poem. The catalog of craftsmen covers not only the length and breadth of the American continent but also the large and varied field of American achievement. This poem expresses Whitman's love of America—its vitality, variety, and the massive achievement which is the outcome of the creative endeavor of all its people. It also illustrates Whitman's technique of using catalogs consisting of a list of people.

"Poets to Come"

Whitman, addressing poets of the future, declares that this great "new brood" should awake and "justify" him. Conscious of his philosophical limitations, he says that he can "but write one or two indicative words for the future." Since he can turn only "a casual look" upon these artists of the future, he leaves to them the interpretation of his thoughts.

Whitman's consciousness of the inadequacy of language to express the full extent of his thought is revealed in this poem. He says that he can "advance a moment only to wheel and hurry ack in the darkness." He is aware of the philosophical and metaphysical imperfections of his poetic self. His expectation that future poets will interpret his work for posterity clearly shows that he views the poet as a seer and a builder of the bridge spanning time.

"To You"

Whitman tells the stranger that if their paths cross they should communicate with each other: "Why should you not speak to me? And why should I not speak to you?"

This poem is only two lines long but it is significant in the way it deals with the relationship between the poet and the reader. A late (1881) addition to *Leaves of Grass,* it deals with the problems of communication and understanding between the artist and his audience, the author and the reading public—and between people in general. Whitman believes that all men are related—if strangers want to communicate, they should not let artificial barriers stop them.

"Thou Reader"

Whitman says that the reader "throbbest life and pride and love" in the same way as the poet does; therefore, he offers "the following chants" *(Leaves of Grass)* to him.

This poem was added to *Leaves of Grass* in 1881. Even though, like "To You," it is only two lines long, it is important because it conveys Whitman's basic attitude toward his reader. The poet identifies himself with the reader. He emphasizes their common humanity.

"Thou Reader" marks the culmination of the *Inscription* poems. It is notable for its ardor and intensity which, being expressed with such meaningful brevity, make it a fitting prelude to *Leaves of Grass.*

"Song of Myself"

Introduction

This poem had no title in the first (1855) edition of *Leaves of Grass*. In 1856 it was called "A Poem of Walt Whitman, an American" and in 1860 it was simply termed "Walt Whitman." Whitman changed the title to "Song of Myself" in 1881. The changes in the title are significant in indicating the growth of the meaning of the poem.

There are three important themes: the idea of the self, the identification of the self with other selves, and the poet's relationship with the elements of nature and the universe. Houses and rooms represent civilization; perfumes signify individual selves; and the atmosphere symbolizes the universal self. The self is conceived of as a spiritual entity which remains relatively permanent in and through the changing flux of ideas and experiences which constitute its conscious life. The self comprises ideas, experiences, psychological states, and spiritual insights. The concept of self is the most significant aspect of Whitman's mind and art.

To Whitman, the self is both individual and universal. Man has an individual self, whereas the world, or cosmos, has a universal or cosmic self. The poet wishes to maintain the identity of his individual self, and yet he desires to merge it with the universal self, which involves the identification of the poet's self with mankind and the mystical union of the poet with God, the Absolute Self. Sexual union is a figurative anticipation of spiritual union. Thus the poet's ecstasy is both physical and spiritual, and he develops a sense of loving brotherhood with God and with all mankind. Even the most commonplace objects, such as leaves, ants, and stones, contain the infinite universe.

"Song of Myself" is a good example of the stylistic features of *Leaves of Grass*. Whitman's style reflects his individualism. He once wrote to Horace Traubel, his biographer: "I sometimes think the *Leaves* is only a language experiment." Words, for

Whitman, have both a "natural" and a "spiritual" significance. Colloquial words unite the natural with the spiritual, and therefore he uses many colloquial expressions. He is also fond of using foreign words. The catalog is another special characteristic of Whitman's poetic technique. He uses numerous images, usually drawn from nature, to suggest and heighten the impression of a poetic idea. These images appear to have no clear organization; yet, in effect, they have a basic underlying unity, usually involving a spiritual concept, which gives meaning and coherence to the apparently disconnected images or scenes.

Sections 1-5, lines 1-98

This poem celebrates the poet's self; but, while the "I" is the poet himself, it is, at the same time, universalized. The poet will "sing myself," but "what I assume you shall assume,/For every atom belonging to me as good belongs to you." The poet loafs on the grass and invites his soul to appear. He relates that he was "form'd from this soil," for he was born here, as were his parents, grandparents and great-grandparents. He is thirty-seven years old and "in perfect health." He hopes to continue his celebration of self until his death. He will let nature speak "without check with original energy."

In section 2, the self, asserting its identity, declares its separateness from civilization and its closeness to nature. "Houses and rooms are full of perfume," Whitman says. "Perfumes" are symbols of other individual selves; but outdoors, the earth's atmosphere denotes the universal self. The poet is tempted to let himself be submerged by other individual selves, but he is determined to maintain his individuality.

The poet expresses the joy he feels through his senses. He is enthralled by the ecstasy of his physical sensations. He can enjoy each of the five senses – tasting, hearing, smelling, touching, and seeing – and even more – the process of breathing, the beating of his heart, and "the feeling of health." He invites the reader to "stop this day and night" with him in order to discover "the origin of all poems."

In the third and fourth sections, Whitman chides the "talkers," "trippers," and "askers" for wasting their time discussing "the beginning and the end," and "the latest dates, discoveries, inventions, societies . . . More important is the eternal procreant urge of the world." He prepares himself for the union of his body with his soul: "I witness and wait." As his soul is "clear and sweet," so are all the other parts of his body—and everyone's bodies. "Not an inch . . . is vile, and none shall be less familiar than the rest."

Section 5 is the poet's ecstatic revelation of union with his soul. He has a feeling of fraternity and oneness with God and his fellowmen ("And I know that the hand of God is the promise of my own/And I know that the spirit of God is the brother of my own") and a vision of love ("And...a kelson [an important structural part of a ship] of the creation is love"). This union brings him peace and joy.

Sections 6-19, lines 99-388

Section 6 presents the first significant transition in the poem and introduces the central symbol in "Song of Myself." A child appears with both hands full of leaves from the fields and asks the poet, "*What is the grass?*" The poet at first feels incapable of answering this question but continues thinking about it. He muses that perhaps "the grass is itself a child" or maybe it is "the handkerchief of the Lord." Here the grass is a symbol of the divinity latent in the ordinary, common life of man and it is also a symbol of the continuity inherent in the life-death cycle. No one really dies. Even "the smallest sprout shows there is really no death," that "all goes onward and outward.../And to die is different from what any one supposed."

In Section 7 the poet signifies his universal nature, which finds it "just as lucky to die" as to be born. The universal self finds both "the earth good and the stars good." The poet is part of everyone around him. He sees all and condemns nothing.

Sections 8-16 consist of a catalog of all that the poet sees—people of both sexes, all ages, and all conditions, in many different walks of life, in the city and in the country, by the mountain and by the sea. Even animals are included. And the poet not only loves them all, he is part of them all:

> And these tend inward to me, and I tend outward to them,
> And such as it is to be of these more or less I am,
> And of these one and all I weave the song of myself.

Section 17 again refers to the universality of the poet—his thoughts are "the thoughts of all men in all ages and lands." Sections 18 and 19 salute all members of humanity.

Grass, a central symbol of this epic poem, suggests the divinity of common things. The nature and significance of grass unfold the themes of death and immortality, for grass is symbolic of the ongoing cycle of life present in nature, which assures each man of his immortality. Nature is an emblem of God, for God's eternal presence in it is evident everywhere. Grass is the key to the secrets of man's relationship with the Divine. It indicates that God is everything and everything is God.

These sections deal with the themes of God, life, death, and nature. Their primary aim is to reveal the nature of the poet's journey through life and the spiritual knowledge which he strives for along the way. They reveal an essential element in a mystical experience—the awakening of the poet's self. "Song of Myself" is a poetical expression of that mystical experience. It arises out of a belief that it is possible to achieve communion with God through contemplation and love, without the medium of human reason. It is a way of attaining knowledge of spiritual truths through intuition. Sections 1 to 5 concern the poet's entry into a mystical state, while sections 6-16 describe the awakening of the poet's self to his own universality.

Sections 20-25, lines 389-581

The poet declares that all he says of himself the reader is to say of his own self, "else it were time lost listening to me." He declares himself to be "solid and sound," "deathless," and "august," and, while no one is better than he, no one is worse, either. In section 21, Whitman proclaims himself "the poet of the Body" and also "the poet of the Soul." He is a poet of pleasures and pain, and of men and women. Calling to the earth, he thanks it for giving him love, which he answers with love: "Prodigal, you have given me love—therefore I to you give love!/O unspeakable passionate love." In section 22 the poet reveals that he also loves the sea. He feels at one with it ("I am integral with you") for it has as many aspects and moods as he has. He is the poet of both good and evil: "I am not the poet of goodness only, I do not decline to be the poet of wickedness also"; the two qualities complement each other. In section 23 the poet affirms his acceptance of "Reality." He salutes scientists but, he admits, "your facts...are not my dwelling."

Section 24 presents some of Whitman's basic tenets. He calls himself a "kosmos." The word "kosmos," meaning a universe, is significant and amounts to a renewed definition of the poet's self as one who loves all people. Through him, "many long dumb voices" of prisoners, slaves, thieves, and dwarfs—all of those whom "the others are down upon"—are articulated and transfigured. He also speaks of lust and the flesh, for each part of the body is a miracle: "The scent of these arm-pits aroma finer than prayer." In section 25 Whitman dwells on the comprehensive range of the poet's power. He declares that "with the twirl of my tongue I encompass world and volumes of world. Speech is the twin of my vision." He must speak, for he cannot contain all that he has to say; and yet "writing and talk do not prove me." What he is can be seen in his face.

The poet's self-appraisal is the keynote of sections 20-25. He describes himself as gross and mystical. He feels he is part of all that he has met and seen. He is essentially a poet of balance, since he accepts both good and evil in his cosmos. His awareness of the universe, or cosmic consciousness, is expressed when he calls himself "a kosmos," invoking a picture of the harmony of the universe. He accepts all life, naked and bare, noble and ignoble, refined and crude, beautiful and ugly, pleasant and painful. The physical and the spiritual both are aspects of his vision, which has an organic unity like the unity of the body and the soul. Whitman realizes that the physical as well as the spiritual are aspects of the Divine. The culmination of the poet's experience of self is the ecstacy of love. Contemplating the meaning of grass in terms of mystical experience, he understands that all physical phenomena are as deathless as the grass.

These chants express various stages of the poet's mystical experience of his self. The first stage may be termed the "Awakening of Self"; the second, the "Purification of Self." Purification involves an acceptance of the body and all its functions. This acceptance reflects the poet's goal to achieve mystical experience through physical reality. This is in opposition to the puritanical view of purification through mortification of the flesh. In Whitman's philosophy, the self is purified not through purgation but through acceptance of the physical. Man should free himself from his traditional sense of sin. The mystical experience paves the way for the merging of physical reality with a universal reality.

Whitman is representative of all humanity because, he says, the voices of diverse people speak through him—voices of men, animals, and even insects. To him, all life is a miracle of beauty. Sections 20-25 close on a note of exaltation of the poet's power of expression, although they indicate that his deeper self is beyond expression.

Sections 26-38, lines 582-975

The poet resolves to listen and be receptive to all sounds. The sounds are familiar: the "bravuras of birds," the "bustle of growing wheat," and "the sound of the human voice." Soon they reach a high pitch and the poet is ecstatic at this "music." Sections 27-30 reveal that the sense of touch also brings the poet joy. Indeed, the poet's sense of touch is extremely acute. At times he is overwhelmed by it, and he asks, "Is this then a touch? quivering me to a new identity." The emphasis is on his search for an individuality, an aspect of his evolving self. He will end his quest for being in an affirmation of his body's sensory awareness. With all his senses, the poet responds to existence and living, "the puzzle of puzzles... that we call Being."

The poet's senses convince him that there is significance in everything, no matter how small. Sections 31-33 contain a catalog of the infinite wonders in small things. He believes, for example, that "a leaf of grass is no less than the journey-work of the stars" and "the narrowest hinge in my hand puts to scorn all machinery," for all things are part of the eternal wonder of life and therefore even "the soggy clods shall become lovers and lamps." He, himself, incorporates an unending range of things, people, and animals. Now he understands the power of his vision which ranges everywhere: "I skirt sierras, my palms cover continents,/I am afoot with my vision." Especially in sections 34-36, he identifies himself with every person, dead or living, and relates his involvement with the various phases of American history. Realizing his relationship to all this makes him feel, as he states in section 38, "replenish'd with supreme power, one of an average unending procession."

In the earlier chants, the accent was on observation; in this sequence it is on what "I" am or what "I" am becoming. Whitman develops a kind of microscopic vision in the way he glorifies the details of the commonplace. The poet's experience is ecstatic; his joy comes to him through his senses, and the physical enjoyment suggests a sexual union as the culmination of this experience of ecstasy. The catalog of people and places is an attempt to give a feeling of universal scope. Ordinary life becomes permeated with mystical significance. The poet identifies himself with every being and every object, and this identification forms an integral part of his concept of what "I" am. The process of identification arises out of the belief that the poet's soul is a part of the universal soul and therefore should seek union with it.

Whitman also discusses the relative properties of the body and the soul. He finds that the body has value, for it leads man to a unified self, a purified combination of the body and the soul. The poet praises the primitive life of animals (section 32) because they have achieved this union—they are born pure. In sections 33-37, Whitman experiences a spiritual illumination, passing through suffering, despair, and the dark night of the soul to finally achieve purification. His self, purified, comprehends the Divine Reality, the "transcendental self." Transcendentalism is a word with varied meanings, but in Whitman's poetry it implies beliefs based on intuitional philosophy which transcend, or go beyond, ordinary experience. Human reason can deal reliably with phenomena, but there is a world beyond phenomena, and this world is approached through faith and intuition. Transcendentalists tried to receive their inspiration at first hand from the Divine Power. Their God was sometimes called the Over-Soul. Whitman's God revealed Himself in nature. The poet's self, inspired by his insights, venerates God, the Divine Reality, who embodies the transcendental self.

Sections 39-41, lines 976-1053

These three sections express the idea of the poet as a sort of superman, flowing through life and the world doing good. He transforms the common into the Divine. In this process, the "common modes" assume "new forms." He answers the call of the needy and the despairing and even becomes a healer to the dying: "To any one dying, thither I speed/...Let the physician and the priest go home." He would seize "the descending man and raise him with resistless will.../By God, you shall not go down! hang your whole weight upon me."

In section 41 the poet assumes the role of the prophet of a new religion, incorporating all religions:

> Taking myself the exact dimensions of Jehovah,
> Lithographing Kronos, Zeus his son, and Hercules
> his grandson,
> Buying drafts of Osiris, Isis, Belus, Brahma, Buddha,
> In my portfolio placing Manito loose, Allah on a leaf,
> the crucifix engraved.

He declares that all men are divine and possess powers of revelation equal to any god's. The poet denies significance to old gods because God is to be found in all men. He says, "The supernatural is of no account," meaning that the Divine is here on earth for all men, who must only become ready to accept this divinity.

"The friendly and flowing savage" mentioned in section 39 is a key image which sums up the progression of ideas and feelings in this section. This image combines the idea of the primitive ancestor of man with the figure of Christ. He is a healer, a comforter, and a lover of humanity. He raises men from their deathbeds and imbues them with strength and vision. This Christ-like savage merges with the other identities contained in the total idea of the poet's self. The primitivity of savage man is divine; modern civilized man has lost this divinity but is eager to regain it.

Whitman's chants recall the experience of Indian sages and mystics (the Samadhi) who, on realizing the state of spiritual absorption, are endowed with divine and superhuman power. The poet is conscious of his newly acquired, holy and superhuman power resulting from the union of his self with the Divine.

Sections 42-52, lines 1054-1347

"A call in the midst of the crowd,/My own voice, orotund [strong and clear] sweeping and final," says the poet, who assumed the position of prophet while acknowledging his kinship with mankind. He says, "I know perfectly well my own egotism," but he would extend it to include all humanity and bring "you whoever you are flush with myself." He sees the injustice that prevails in society but recognizes that the reality beneath the corruption is deathless: "The weakest and shallowest is deathless with me."

In section 43, Whitman states that he does not despise religion but asserts that his own faith embraces all "worship ancient and modern." He practices all religions and even looks beyond them to "what is yet untried." This unknown factor will not fail the suffering and the dead. In the next section, the poet expresses his desire to "launch all men and women...into the Unknown" by stripping them of what they already know. In this way he will show them their relationship with eternity. "We have thus far exhausted trillions of winters and summers,/There are trillions ahead, and trillions ahead of them." The poet is conscious of the confrontation of his self with limitless time and limitless space and realizes that he and his listeners are products of ages past and future.

Section 45 again deals with eternity and the ages of man. Everything leads to the mystical union with God, the "great Camerado." In section 46, the poet launches himself on the "perpetual journey," urging all to join him and uttering the warning, "Not I, not any one else can travel that road for you,/You must travel it for yourself." The poet (section 47) says that he is a teacher, but he hopes that those he teaches will learn to assert their own individuality: "He most honors my style who learns under it to destroy the teacher." Section 48 repeats the idea that "the soul is not more than the body," just as "the body is not more than the soul." Not even God is more important than one's self. The poet asks man not to be "curious about God" because God is everywhere and in everything: "In the faces of men and women I see God, and in my own face in the glass."

The poet is not afraid of death. In section 49, he addresses it: "And as to you Death, you bitter hug of mortality, it is idle to try to alarm me." For there is no real death. Men die and are reborn in different forms. He himself has died "ten thousand times before." The poet feels (section 50) there is something that outweighs death, although it is hard for him to put a name to it: "It is form, union, plan—it is eternal life—it is Happiness."

The last two sections are expressions of farewell. "The past and present wilt—I have fill'd them, emptied them,/And proceed to fill my next fold of the future." He knows that his writings have been obscure but sees the paradoxes in his works as natural components in the mysteries of the cosmos: "Do I contradict myself?/Very well then I contradict myself,/(I am large, I contain multitudes.)" The poet can wait for those who will understand him. He tells them, "If you want me again look for me under your boot-soles," for he will have become part of the eternal life cycle. Although it may be difficult to find or interpret him, he will be waiting. "Missing me one place search another,/I stop somewhere waiting for you."

The poet's journey and quest for selfhood have now come full circle. He began by desiring to loaf on the grass and ends by bequeathing himself "to the dirt to grow from the grass I love."

These chants contain many of the important ideas and doctrines of Whitman. The poet brings a new message of faith for the strong and the weak, a belief in the harmony and orderliness of the universe. The poet, noting what has been said about the universe, shows how his own theories, which have a more universal scope, transcend them. Assuming the identity of the Savage-Christ, he delivers a sermon which imagines transcendence of the finite through a union of the individual soul with the Divine Soul. The poet offers to lead men and women "into the unknown"—that is, into transcendent reality. Whitman talks about the self as part of the eternal life process. There is no death, for man is reincarnated time and time again. The poet speaks about man's relation with the moment and with eternity. Eternity is time endless, as is the self.

The poet does not prescribe any fixed pathway to a knowledge of the self; it is for each person to find his own way to make the journey. The poet is not afraid of death because death, too, is a creation of God and through it one may reach God. The culmination of the poet's mystical experience is revealed in his vision of eternal life. Life is neither chaotic nor finite; it is harmonious, reflecting the union of the poet's individual soul with the Divine Soul.

Grass is the central symbol of "Song of Myself," and it represents the divinity contained in all living things. Although no traditional form is apparent, the logical manner in which the poet returns to his image of grass shows that "Song of Myself" was planned to have an order and unity of idea and image.

CHILDREN OF ADAM

A group of fifteen poems in the 1860 version of *Leaves of Grass* was entitled *Enfans d'Adam.* In 1867, these poems, after a few changes, were retitled *Children of Adam.* In the 1892 edition, the group consists of sixteen poems.

The major themes of *Children of Adam* are procreation and physical love between man and woman. The themes are dealt with through imagery rich in Christian tradition. Whitman uses many Christian concepts in his own unique way to express his individual precepts for mankind.

Fundamental to Christian belief is the story of the Fall of Man, interpreted either literally or symbolically. Adam and Eve, falling prey to Satan's temptation, disobeyed the divine command and ate the forbidden fruit of knowledge. This act of disobedience resulted in Original Sin, the inheritance of humanity. Man is therefore a born sinner, and his only hope of salvation lies in the grace of God, attained through Jesus Christ.

Whitman reverses this traditional Christian tenet. He asserts that it is not Adam but Adam's children who have really lost the Garden of Eden. Adam's children can regain this lost paradise not by denying the flesh, which had been a Puritan belief, but by accepting it. Man will then be reborn through this glorification of his body, for the human body is as sacred as the spirit. Thus, man is not born debased as a result of Original Sin. He should be proud of his heritage and of the "Adamic" in him.

The theme of procreation in these poems was revolutionary at the time of their first publication. Whitman thinks that procreation is a creative act, an act of spiritual regeneration. Man finds fulfillment in sex and should thus rejoice in it, for it is only through physical love that man can take his place in the cycle of life. And it is only through spiritual regeneration that man can complete his quest—and the full, uninhibited experience of sex is seen as the first step to spiritual regeneration.

"To the Garden of the World"

Man endeavors to ascend to the Garden of Eden again. But only through love can he achieve this goal. Physical love gives meaning to man's life and the body lends substance to his existence. The poet is ready for rebirth. Life seems beautiful and wondrous to him and the quivering fire in his limbs prepares him for physical love. He is content. Eve (woman) is with him: "By my side or back of me Eve following,/Or in front, and I following her just the same."

"To the Garden the World" is the opening poem of the *Children of Adam* group. It celebrates the physical love between man and woman. Love is conceived of as a cosmic force which will help restore man to his lost paradise. Whitman reverses traditional Christian teachings (derived from the story of Genesis in the Old Testament) to make the children of Adam proud, rather than ashamed, of their heritage. The poet recreates for modern man the ideal of sexual innocence in the joy of Adam before the Fall. Man shouldn't treat the body as a source of the immoral, but accept it as a necessary medium of spiritual regeneration. Whitman visualizes human beings who will rejoice in the physical relationships between men and women. The poet's body shakes with physical desires and his phrase "I peer and penetrate" has an obvious sexual implication. The modern Eve is either by man's side, or leading, or following—this implies Whitman's belief that women should enjoy equality with men.

"Spontaneous Me"

The spontaneous and instinctive force within the poet is nature. The rising sun, the "blossoms of the mountain ash" on the hillside, and the grass are all parts of nature, as is "the friend I am happy with." The "real poems" are inside man himself. These "poems of the privacy of the night" are sexual. Love and sexual passion and the human body are poetry. Man is compared to "the hairy wild-bee" that "gripes the full-grown lady-flower, curves upon her with amorous firm legs." All things are involved in this sexual feeling, nature and man alike. The young man who "wakes deep at night" with "the strange half-welcome pangs" is ashamed and angry. But why should man, who is just one part of this process, think himself indecent when birds and animals do not? Paternity and maternity are chaste. Therefore the poet is proud of the "Adamic" in him (his sexual heritage) and has sworn "the oath of procreation" so that he may "produce boys to fill my place when I am through."

The central idea of the poem is contained in the first line: "Spontaneous me, Nature." The free, uninhibited sexual passion within man is indeed natural. Whitman presents two aspects of nature. The human aspect is shown in "the arm of my friend hanging idly over my shoulder" and in "two sleepers at night lying close together as they sleep." The non-human aspect is exemplified in the "hillside whiten'd with blossoms," "the hairy wild-bee," "the wet of woods," and "the dead leaf." Whitman includes all the senses of man, although the emphasis is primarily on the sense of touch.

The poet has taken a vow of procreation. He is eager to give full and free play to his instincts and desires. In this he plays the part of an Adamic man. The sexual images follow each other naturally—the wet of wood, the walnut trunk, the apples—in keeping with the stream-of-consciousness of the poem itself. Thus the phallic is linked with the poetic and the spiritual.

Whitman, in presenting his images, makes use of many equivalents. Objects of nature and of human life are simultaneously presented to show the poet's idea of nature within him. The cluster of images reinforces the idea and the title of the poem. (The poem was originally entitled "Bunch," which expressed the idea of the cluster of images.)

"Ages and Ages Returning at Intervals"

The poet becomes Adam himself. He returns to the earth to chant "lusty, phallic" songs. In the West, home of the new Garden of Eden, the great cities call him. He offers his songs and himself, bathing both in the sex which issues forth from his body.

Merging his identity with Adam, the poet takes it as his mission to spread the gospel of sex. The joy of the sexual experience is equated with the ecstasy of a spiritual or mystical experience. The image of bathing in sex is reminiscent of the sacrament of Baptism.

The poem is structured in a pattern of heightening and declining stresses. The initial lines have few stresses, the lines in the central part have more, the closing lines again have few stresses. The power of sex is described in liquid consonants which show Whitman's onomatopoeic skill, his ability to use words whose sounds suggest their meaning. "Deliriate" is the poet's own invention; it means the process of bringing about a temporary state of mental and sexual excitement.

"As Adam Early in the Morning"

The poet feels as if he is Adam as he walks forth in the morning after a refreshing sleep. He asks the reader to look at him and to touch him without fear: "Touch me, touch the palm of your hand to my body as I pass,/Be not afraid of my body."

This, the concluding poem of *Children of Adam,* contains the central thought of Whitman in this group, that Adam continually returns to the earth in the shape of modern man. He is aware of the beauty, strength, and vitality of his body. The central verb in this poem is "touch," which is a means of sensory perception, sexual enjoyment, and spiritual fulfillment. There is an image of Christ in this Adam—his touch contains the promise of healing diseased society. The poet appeals to the reader to listen to him as he expounds his message of joyous, natural sex.

CALAMUS

Calamus, the name of a plant, was the title given to a group of poems in the 1860 edition of *Leaves.* The rather phallic-leafed plant may suggest comradeship or "adhesiveness." Whitman was interested in phrenology, a pseudo-science dealing with character as supposedly revealed by a study of skull formation. Adhesiveness is a term used in phrenology to refer to emotional comradeship between men.

The *Calamus* poems (which Whitman originally thought of calling *Live-Oak*), thirty-nine in number, are marked by emotional intensity and eloquent expression. They also raise the question of Whitman's life in relation to his poetry.

Whitman makes use of the calamus as a many-faceted metaphor. It stands for "athletic love" and for varying degrees of attachment between men. Its different connotations arise from the varied levels of the love between comrades—the resilience and depth of that love. Calamus grows in various shapes and forms and its variety accords with the diversity of love between men.

"In Paths Untrodden"

The poet desires to travel the untrodden paths which previously were denied him by "all the standards" and "conformities." In a "secluded spot," far "away from the clank of the world," the poet can at last, in his "forty-first year," "respond as I would not dare elsewhere." He resolves to sing songs of "manly attachment" and "types of athletic love," and "to celebrate the need of comrades."

The untrodden paths to which Whitman refers are unknown and unpredictable human behavior. They also indicate the free-thinking of skeptics and dissenters. The calamus grows in a secluded place near a pond, which suggests serenity and peace. Calamus gives joy to the poet's spirit which, until then, fed on mere materialistic pleasures. He had suppressed his spiritual impulses, which should have found full expression; now, at last, he begins to walk those unused paths. It is a journey of self-discovery. He is now in communion with nature, and his inmost being responds freely. He thus realizes different levels of athletic love and manly attachment. The significance of the term "athletic" probably lies in strong, physical love; "manly attachment" suggests the affectionate relationship between comrades. But both these emotions are essentially spiritual.

"Scented Herbage of My Breast"

The fragrant "herbage of my breast" suggests the poet's poems, which are called "leaves." The poet's death will not destroy his thoughts; the leaves will continue to grow from his grave—for the leaves are "blossoms of my blood" and unfold the poet's heart. Some few passers-by will notice the leaves and "inhale [their] faint odor." The leaves make the poet "think of death." Death and love are both beautiful: the poet does not know whether he prefers death or life. He thinks "these leaves" (his poetry) carry the same message as does death.

The poet declares that he stifled his inmost being far too long and far too much. He now is "determin'd to unbare this broad breast." His doctrine of love and comradeship will find "immortal reverberations through the States" and be "an example to lovers." Love and death are "folded inseparably together." Death is the "real reality" which waits for all and which will "dissipate this entire show of appearance."

The title "Scented Herbage of My Breast" evokes, for one thing, a concrete image of a strong, robust chest. The theme of love and death is concretized by this image. The herbage is fragrant; it suggests the spiritual emanation of love. The breast contains the heart, poetically the source of love. The image of herbage is later transformed into "leaves" (poems), which future generations will read. "Tomb-leaves" symbolize the idea of the immortality of man: leaves continue to flourish on tombs and assert the supremacy of the principle of life in death. "Perennial roots" signify the heart, of which the leaf is the artistic expression.

The calamus plant suggests many qualities of spiritual love. The poet introduces many variations on the significance of leaves: they represent the calamus plant, the hair on the breast, the grass on the grave, the pages of a book of poems, and the growth of spiritual love. At last, death brings men to the "real reality"—spiritual love. Thus manly, or athletic, love is another aspect of spiritual love.

"Whoever You Are Holding Me Now in Hand"

The poet gives a "fair warning" to his would-be followers, the readers who now hold his words in their hands: "I am not what you supposed, but far different." He desires to know who would become "a candidate for my affections." Those who would follow him will have to abandon conformity. The poet cannot reveal himself in libraries. But if he is alone with his companion, "here to put your lips upon mine I permit you,/With the comrade's long-dwelling kiss or the new husband's kiss,/For I am the new husband and I am the comrade," a touch will reveal his meaning, but if one tries to understand him through the mind alone, he "will certainly elude you."

"Whoever You Are Holding Me Now in Hand" is significant for its direct communication with the reader. It deals with a love which is physical and spiritual at the same time. Whitman's animalism is part of his sense of concrete reality. He believes that the love of comrades is physical and procreative and therefore is an essential part of cosmic consciousness, or the awareness of the universe, which is spiritual.

"When I Heard at the Close of the Day"

The poet says that he was not happy on the day he heard that his work was praised "in the capitol," nor was he pleased when "his plans were accomplish'd." But he felt especially happy when he rose in the morning in perfect health, wandered over the beach, saw the sun and the cool waters, and remembered that his "lover was on his way." And on the night when "the one I love most lay sleeping by me under the same cover in the cool night," he was happy.

This is really a sonnet in free verse. Although a true sonnet has fourteen lines and is usually in iambic pentameter, the lyricism here is sonnet-like. The scenes of "the full moon" and "the beach" are fine examples of synonymous descriptions. The poet builds up the details which are accentuated in the depiction of personal relationships and love. The movement of the verse is rhythmic. The reference to the "plaudits in the capitol" is possibly based on the favorable review of *Leaves of Grass* in the *National Intelligencer* (Washington, D.C., February 18, 1856).

"Are You the New Person Drawn Toward Me?"

The poet speaks to a new admirer, warning him, "I am surely far different from what you suppose." His faithfulness and tolerance are but a facade. Is the person "advancing on real ground toward a real heroic man," or is this mere "maya" or illusion?

Whitman knew the complexity of love and the relationship between master and disciple. He warns his disciples that he is very different from their image of him. This warning is the only positive statement in this poem; the rest is made up of rhetorical questions dealing with the poet's "facade."

"Not Heat Flames Up and Consumes"

The poet declares that the flames within burn him more than actual heat, and that his consuming passion "for his love whom I love" is quicker than air and tide. His soul, "borne through the open air," is irresistibly drawn to his friend.

The imagery here—of "sea-waves," the "delicious and dry" air, the "tide... seeking something," the "rain-emitting clouds"—is sexually expressive. The poet feels that his love is as irresistible and mystical as are the forces of nature. The self of the poet is shown floating on the open air and this image suggests the mystical merger of man's soul with the Divine Soul. Calamus love thus finally develops into a mystical union.

"I Saw in Louisiana a Live-Oak Growing"

The poet observed an oak tree in Louisiana which stood alone and whose dark leaves were delightful. The oak was rough, unyielding, and lusty—it reminded the poet of himself, though he wondered "how it could utter joyous leaves" all alone, without a friend—he would not be able to. The poet broke off a twig and carried it to his room. To him it seemed a strange "token... of manly love." And still he wonders how it could utter joyous messages through its leaves "without... a lover near."

The twig is a phallic symbol. Even the live oak itself approximates the phallic and thus suggests manly love. Physical love is as elementary as the oak tree itself, but its luxuriant growth is an organic metaphor for the development of manly love in the region of the spirit. Whitman is surprised that the tree is able to express itself so luxuriantly alone—he could not write his "leaves," or poems, without companionship.

This poem has only thirteen lines and it has neither a regular rhythmic nor a formal stanzaic pattern, but it has an affinity with the sonnet because of its lyricism. "I Saw in Louisiana a Live-Oak Growing" is a key poem of the *Calamus* group.

"Full of Life Now"

The poet is in his fortieth year and is "full of life." Yet when generations of the future will read his *Leaves*, "I that was visible am become invisible." He speaks to these unborn readers who are seeking him. He tells them that perhaps he is with them.

"Full of Life Now" is the last poem of the *Calamus* group. The poet presents his ideas on the phases of his development from the physical to the spiritual, from the world of manly love to the world of poetry. His past is dark, but his future is bright because he has grown into a poet. His growth as a poet establishes a link between him and his future readers, and he is with them, though apart. He moves away from the seen world to the unseen universe which is the essence of his spiritual life and experience.

"Crossing Brooklyn Ferry"

This poem was originally called "Sun-Down Poem" (1856), and the present title was given it in 1860. It was substantially revised in 1881.

The major image in the poem is the ferry. It symbolizes continual movement, backward and forward, a universal motion in space and time. The ferry moves on, from a point of land, through water, to another point of land. Land and water thus form part of the symbolistic pattern of the poem. Land symbolizes the physical; water symbolizes the spiritual. The circular flow from the physical to the spiritual connotes the dual nature of the universe. Dualism, in philosophy, means that the world is ultimately composed of, or explicable in terms of, two basic entities, such as mind and matter. From a moral point of view, it means that there are two mutually antagonistic principles in the universe—good and evil. In Whitman's view, both the mind and the spirit are realities and matter is only a means which enables man to realize this truth. His world is dominated by a sense of good, and evil has a very subservient place in it. Man, in Whitman's world, while overcoming the duality of the universe, desires fusion with the spirit. In this attempt, man tries to transcend the boundaries of space and time.

The ferry symbolizes this spatial and temporal movement. It is also associated with the groups of men and women who ride it, who have ridden it, and who will ride it. The coming together of these men and women symbolizes the spiritual unity of men in this world.

The poet first addresses the elements—the tide, the clouds, and the sun—saying, "I see you face to face." He next observes the crowds of men and women on the ferryboats: "How curious you are to me" he says, for he thinks of these people in relation to those who "shall cross from shore to shore years hence." The poet meditates on the relationships between the various generations of men.

This first section establishes the setting of the poem. The poet is on the bank, and he observes the ferry as well as the passengers, whom he expands to symbolize the large united self of mankind. The tide, the cloud, and the sun become integral characters in this spiritual drama between the poet and the elements. The poet first responds to natural objects and then to people with the ultimate aim of bringing about an imaginative fusion between himself and the reader.

In the second section, the men and women on the ferryboat become the eternal "impalpable sustenance" of the poet. He thinks of "the simple, compact, well-join'd scheme" of the universe and believes himself to be "disintegrated yet part of the scheme." He thinks again about all the people of the future who "will enter the gates of the ferry and cross from shore to shore."

The poet thinks about his role in relation to the nature of the universe. To him, the universe seems compact, harmonious, and well-adjusted. He is part of the multitude of men, part of the eternal processes of birth, life, and death. Whitman probes into the future and identifies himself with persons who will cross the river "a hundred years hence." Thus a link is established between the poet and the "others"–including future readers.

In section 3, Whitman declares that neither time nor place really matter, for he is part of this generation and of many generations hence. He speaks to future generations and tells them that their experiences are not new: "I too many and many a time cross'd the river of old,/Watched the Twelfth-month sea-gulls, .../Saw the reflection of the summer sky in the water." He, too, saw the ships arriving, "the sailors at work," and "the flags of all nations." He, too, saw "the fires from the foundry chimneys burning high and glaringly into the night."

This third section reveals the poet's desire to transcend time, place, and distance in order to establish contact with people of future generations. His own experience is similar to that of the reader years from now.

The description of the journey on the river is very vivid. The movement of the day from morning until midnight is parallel to the movement of the poet from one side of the river to another and from the physical to the spiritual.

In section 4, Whitman declares his deep love for the cities, the river, and the people. This section is transitional and marks the beginning of the change of the poet's attitude toward men and objects. For the first time (in this poem) he becomes emotionally involved in his relationships with other people and things. The reference to the future is prophetic and anticipates the growth of spiritual kinship between the poet and the reader.

The poet, in section 5, poses a question about the relationship between himself and the generations to come. Even if there are hundreds of years between them, they are united by things which do not change. He, too, lived in Brooklyn and walked the Manhattan streets. He, too, "felt the curious abrupt questionings" stir within him. He believes that his body, his physical existence, has become a ferry uniting him with all mankind.

Thus section 5 is the central core of the poem. The poet, in seeking his own physical and spiritual identity, endeavors to unite his sensibility with that of his reader. His experience transcends the limits of the Brooklyn ferry and is universalized. His quest now becomes more intellectual than before; the "curious abrupt questionings" are no longer emotional. Wishing to suggest the quality of spiritual unification, Whitman has used the metaphor of a chemical solution: "The float forever held in solution" is the infinite ocean of spiritual life which contains the "potential" of all life. The spiritual solution is the source of one's being. The use of the term "solution" is significant because it indicates the merging of man's existence with his spirit. Spiritually, he is united with future generations and with all of mankind.

In section 6 the poet tells us that he has been engulfed by the same "dark patches" of doubt which have engulfed the reader. His best actions have appeared "blank" and "suspicious." He, too, has known "what it was to be evil" and he, too, "blabb'd, blush'd, resented, lied, stole, grudg'd,/Had guile, anger, lust, hot wishes I dared not speak." But life, finally, is what we make it—"the same old role...as great as we like,/Or as small as we like." The "old knot of contrariety" the poet has experienced refers to Satan and his evil influence on man, which creates the condition of contraries, of moral evil and good in human life. The poet suffered from these evil influences, as have all men. So, the poet implies, do not feel alone because you have been this way—one must accept both the pure and the impure elements of life.

In section 7, the poet, addressing his reader, says: "Closer yet I approach you." The poet is thinking as much of the reader-yet-unborn as the reader, while he reads, is now thinking of the poet. And perhaps now, though he cannot be seen, the poet is watching the reader. The poet is trying to establish a link between himself and his future readers. The link is not only of location (as on the ferry) but of thought processes as well. These thought processes will eventually lead to the mystical fusion between the poet and the reader.

In section 8, Whitman describes the beauty of the Manhattan harbor, the sunset on the river, the seagulls, and the twilight. He realizes that the bonds between himself and other people are subtle but enduring. Between himself and the person who "looks in my face" is the subtlest bond. The union between himself and others cannot be understood in ordinary terms, by teaching, or by preaching—it is more mystical and intuitive. Recalling the scene of the river and the people with whom he was associated, he evokes the spiritual bond that links man with his fellow men. The reference to fusion ("which fuses me into you now") is the basic ideal the poet sought in the beginning. The union with the reader is mystical and beyond the bounds of rational thought or philosophy.

In section 9, the poet invokes the river to flow "with the flood-tide," the clouds to shower upon him and the other passengers, and the "tall masts of Mannahatta" to stand up. He calls on everything—the bird, the sky, and the water—to keep on fulfilling their function with splendor, for everything is part of the universal life flow. The poet desires that the "eternal float of solution" should suspend itself everywhere. Physical objects, like "dumb, beautiful ministers," wait for their union with the poet's soul. Thus, at the end of the poem, Whitman addresses himself to material objects, which are also part of the life process because they are useful to man.

This section is significant in that it uses the language of incantation. The poet invokes the images of his experiences to suggest the flowing of time. The physical existence of man is like a ferry plying between the two shores of mortality and immortality. He and his fancy (his imagination) use objects to express the idea of the search for the eternal beyond the transient. This search, or the function of fancy, is exemplified by the ferry ride which moves from a point in the physical world to a destination in the spiritual world. This journey of the spirit can take place easily in a universe which is harmonious and well adjusted.

"Song of the Broad-Axe"

"Song of the Broad-Axe" expresses Walt Whitman's fundamental ideas and his basic means of poetic expression through the use of complex symbolism. Initially the broadaxe signifies the constructive and creative spirit of the pioneers, their great zest and initiative, which led to the opening of the West in America. But it also implies and embodies the processes of mystic evolution. This evolution will ultimately assert the supremacy of good over evil. Individuality is the hallmark of man in Whitman's view, and yet he believes man to be part of the vast mass of mankind. This view of man extends to Whitman's notion of America and the American. The symbol of the broadaxe thus becomes the symbol of the growth and development of American society and of America, which is multifarious and yet a single nation. The broadaxe exemplifies the unity in diversity which is a significant quality of American society. It also symbolizes the mystic growth of man which inspires and sustains him and civilization in general.

The broadaxe is introduced in the first section. It is a "shapely" weapon, "naked," and pale. Its head is derived from the bowels of Mother Earth. Its wood is likened to limb and flesh. The axe is leaning on the grass: "To be lean'd and to lean on" are its primary functions.

The broadaxe is the principal image throughout this dramatic poem, and its various aspects are presented in quick succession. It is first seen as a physical object. It has the shape of a weapon.

Next, it is given a human identity as it is linked to its "mother's bowels." Third, the axe is identified with nature, as its head is compared to a leaf. The reference to "head" implies human attributes, too—specifically, the power of thought.

In the second section the poet extends his welcome to "all earth's lands" of whatever kind—lands whereon grow the pine, oak, lemon, fig, wheat, or grape. The lands which produce cotton are as welcome as those which yield potatoes. The "lands of mines" are also welcome; it is they which yield the ore to produce the axe. This description of the diversity of lands stresses the relationship between the axe and the earth. The earth is desolate in part, but the axe is always creative. The poet also repeats the principle of unity in diversity in his description of various types of lands. Some lands are productive while others are desolate and barren, yet all are parts of the earth. All the lands share in the poet's all-inclusive vision.

The third section of the poem tells of the many uses of the broadaxe. The axe helps man to build a "sylvan hut" and to get "the space clear'd for a garden." And it also builds cities. It represents a beginning, "the outset anywhere," the spirit of those "who sought a New England and found it." It is of use to "the butcher in the slaughter-house, the hands aboard schooners," and the "lumbermen in their winter camp." The poet describes a house being built, ships being built, and "the blazing fire at night" being enjoyed—all because of the axe. The poet describes how the broadaxe is made. Then he talks about the past, when primitive workers used the axe for building and when soldiers used it in combat. The broadaxe was used in the sack and seige of cities in ancient times. It symbolized "the hell of war, the cruelties of creeds," and the lust for power among men.

The "Song of the Broad-Axe" reveals Whitman's concept of mystic evolution. In this mystical process, good is mixed with evil, but good will triumph ultimately. The broadaxe is associated with the elements of darkness, but ultimately the spirit of the pioneers which it represents will assert itself.

This third section is a fine example of Whitman's use of the catalog; in a series of pictures, a pageant of users and uses of the axe is presented. The poet's intention is to demonstrate "the beauty of all adventurous and daring persons"—the ordinary people who built this country. Whitman's ability to paint word pictures is revealed in the diversity of the scenes describing these workmen, scenes in which he includes both past and present. The uses of the broadaxe are destructive as well as constructive. "The crash and cut away of connecting wood-work" shows the destructive use of the axe (in this case, firefighting); in addition, ancient warriors used the axe as a weapon. But whether it is used to create or destroy, the axe is effective essentially because it sets the world of action in motion and in this way participates in the mystic evolution of the universe.

Section 4 celebrates "muscle and pluck forever." These are the sources of power behind the action of the axe. Whitman asks rhetorical questions: "What do you think endures?" Do great cities, manufacturing states, constitutions, or armaments endure? The answer is that these are not important in themselves and will not endure unless they are expressions of "personal qualities." The whole world is a show and "the show passes." Only the city that is great, "which has the greatest men and women"—even if it consists only of ragged huts—that city will be "the greatest city in the whole world."

In this section there is a shift of emphasis from the material to the spiritual. Action "invigorates life," but it also "invigorates death." The axe is not even mentioned in this section, but it is indirectly associated with physical action. Physical action and spiritual vigor are interlinked and are both forms of human endeavor. The poet's view that "the living" and "the dead" advance in their own way shows the mystic progression of time and the unfolding of evolution. What endures is the action of great men and women. It is only the great (symbolized by the spirit of the broadaxe) who give meaning and spiritual significance to actions and events in this world.

In section 5 the poet explains the constituents and characteristics of a great city. A great city is not made merely of long docks, tall and costly buildings, and good libraries and schools, nor is it the "place of the most numerous population." A real city is a place "where the slave ceases"; where "fierce men and women pour forth"; where "equanimity is illustrated in affairs"; and where "speculations on the soul are encouraged." The great city stands where "the cleanliness of the sexes stands" and where the "faithfulest friends" stand. Such a city is beloved by its "orators and bards" and "loves them in return."

In enumerating the characteristics and elements which make a great city, Whitman is restating some of his fundamental ideas—for instance, his opposition to slavery, his belief in "inside authority" and in the "cleanliness of the sexes." These beliefs are central to Whitman's credo and are expressed in other poems, such as "Song of Myself" and the poems in *Children of Adam.*

Whitman says, in section 6, that "a defiant deed" defeats all "beggarly" arguments and conquers "the materials of cities." A "strong being" who embodies the power of the race is the master of old materials and customs. The value of a community is therefore represented by its strong men and women rather than by its respectability or money-making capacity. Without strong people, what use are "theology...traditions [and] statute-books"?

Whitman does not think that the strong person is a tyrant; he is, rather, a spiritual leader. This leader raises his voice and power against all materialistic domination, and "the floridness of the materials of cities" is overcome by his innate spiritual energy. He is a nonconformist since he goes against the prevailing tide of materialistic gain. He is thus a representative of the spirit of the broadaxe.

Section 7 describes a barren landscape wherein the miners work. The miners and smiths produce the axe. The broadaxe has served man and mankind over the centuries. It has "served the Hebrew, the Persian, the most ancient Hindustanee," as well as "the druids" and "the hardy pirates of the Baltic." It has "served all great works on land and all great works on the sea." It has served the living and the dead.

Whereas in earlier sections the broadaxe symbolized individuality, in this section it stands for unity. It unites the ancient age with the modern age. It serves the ends of pleasure as well as those of war. It also serves the dead, since it is used for making coffins. Thus it is a link between two worlds. Whitman emphasizes the unifying role of the broadaxe in the history of civilization.

In section 8, "the European headsman" is described as "mask'd, clothed in red," and leaning "on a ponderous axe." His axe, fresh from slaughter, drips with the blood of his victims. The poet imagines these martyrs, including people who rose in revolt and "died for the good cause." Now the scaffold is empty, and Whitman sees "the headsman withdraw and become useless." The axe is the "mighty and friendly emblem of power" of a new race—the Americans.

Whitman's faith in the nineteenth-century concept of progress through continual human endeavor is revealed in this section. The dawn of democracy was preceded by the darkness of feudal oppression and injustice. Man's advance toward democracy was marked by intense struggles in which many valiant fighters lost their lives. But they had faith in their cause, which eventually succeeded. The broadaxe becomes the sign and symbol of this evolutionary process. It becomes the "emblem of the power," says Whitman, "of my own race."

In section 9, Whitman describes how "the axe leaps" to its work and the forests surrender to its power. The axe builds citadels, academies, ceilings, organs, windows, panels, chairs, workboxes, "boat, frame, and what not." Hospitals and steamboats are built with the aid of the axe. Many people use the axe.

There are three clear divisions in this section. First, the role of the axe in construction work is concrete proof of the advances of man and civilization. This program is especially relevant to American society since "capitols of States" are its visible proof. The forests are "solid," the utterances are "fluid," and their combination indicates the coming together of the material and the spiritual. Second, attention is focused on the multifarious users of the axe, whose "shapes," the forms it makes, are described. Third, the poet speaks of the importance of communications, like bridges, to suggest another utility of the axe. The idea of transportation, or passage, is significant in Whitman's poetry.

Whitman continues, in section 10, his description of the shapes formed by the axe. The image of the "coffin-shape" is followed by that of "the bride's bed" and "the babe's cradle." The axe also creates roofs over happy homes, such as that of "the well-married young man and woman." On the other hand, "the shape of the prisoner's place in the court-room" and the couch of the "adulterous unwholesome couple" are also products of the axe. The axe produces "the door that admits good news and bad news."

The function and the role of the broadaxe characterize the whole cycle of life and death, from the cradle to the coffin. The axe symbolizes the coexistence of good and evil. For example, the picture of the chaste wife is contrasted with that of the adulterous couple. The symbol of the door is morally ambivalent; it is characterized by both good and evil. In this way the axe becomes a complex moral symbol.

In section 11, the shape of a woman rises. She is a striking figure. She moves among the "gross and soil'd" yet is not soiled by them. She is "considerate," "friendly," and "the best belov'd," and she has no fears. She maintains her poise despite "quarrels" and "smutty expressions" because she is self-possessed. She is "strong" because "she too is a law of Nature."

This impressive personality is Whitman's New Woman. She is highly individualistic and yet well adjusted to the poet's concept of a democratic society. But her relationship with her environment is not always harmonious, although her self-possession prevents evil from harming her. Through this woman, the motif of the broadaxe as a symbol of mystic evolution is realized and strengthened.

In section 12, the poet refers to the rise of the "shapes of Democracy," the outcome of centuries of human endeavor. These shapes will inspire other shapes; eventually, the democratic shapes will cover the whole world.

This is the culmination of the poet's vision of the axe: it has now become the symbol of the total and full democracy. The concept of the "shape" is contrasted with that of formlessness. The "shape" is creative, purposive, individualistic, and it grows in terms of time and space; it is part of a cycle and also a proof of progress. The poet's vision reveals his concept of democracy and his belief that the whole world will be united in harmony, peace, and love. This is man's dream of the future, and the broadaxe becomes the symbol of that unrealized dream.

"Pioneers! O Pioneers!"

"Pioneers! O Pioneers!" is a paean of praise to the pioneers, those Americans who, by great effort, succeeded in transforming wilderness into civilization. Whitman identifies himself, body and soul, with them and is determined to march on the road to progress. The poet appears as a prophet—like Moses, he will lead the modern Israelites to a new Promised Land.

"Tan-faced children" and "Western youths" are called upon to fell "primeval forests" and to cross rivers and mountains in order to reach the West. Some of these pioneers "droop and die" on their journey. But, cheered on by "all the pulses of the world," the rest will reach their goal.

In this poem it is suggested that the movement of Americans to the West is another way of fulfilling a divine purpose; it is one form of the fruition of mystic evolution, of the material and spiritual progress of man.

"Out of the Cradle Endlessly Rocking"

Out of the ceaselessly rocking cradle of the sea waves, a memory comes back to the poet. He recalls that as a child, he left his bed and "wander'd alone, bareheaded, barefoot" in search of the mystery of life and death. He is a man now but "by these tears a little boy again," and he throws himself on the shore "confronting the waves." He is a "chanter of pains and joys, uniter of here and hereafter," and he uses all his experiences but goes beyond them.

The experience he now recalls is that on the Paumanok seashore one May, when lilacs were in bloom, he observed two mockingbirds, "feather'd guests from Alabama." The female "crouch'd on her nest, silent," and the male went "to and fro near at hand." The birds sang of their love; the words "two together" summed up their existence. One day the female disappeared, "may-be kill'd, unknown to her mate." The male anxiously awaited her. He addressed the wind: "I wait and I wait till you blow my mate to me." His song penetrated the heart of the curious boy who "treasur'd every note," for he understood the meaning of the bird, whom he called his "brother."

The bird's lament, or "aria," affected the boy deeply. Every shadow seemed to the bird the hoped-for shape of his mate reappearing. He had loved, but now "we two [are] together no more."

The notes of the bird were echoed by the moaning sea, "the fierce old mother." To the boy who became the poet, "to the outsetting bard," the sea hinted at secrets. The boy eagerly asked the sea to let him know the ultimate meaning, "the word final, superior to all." Before daybreak the sea whispered to the poet the "delicious word death.../Death, death."

In this experience the boy attempted to fuse the vision of the sea with that of the bird, and this knowledge marked the beginning of the poet in him. The bird, the solitary singer, was a projection of the boy's consciousness. The sea, like the "old crone rocking the cradle," whispered the key word in his ears.

This poem was first published under the title "A Child's Reminiscence" (1859), was later called "A Word out of the Sea" (1860), and the present, highly symbolic title was given it in 1871. The present title suggests "a word from the sea," and that word is death, which is the second phase in the process of birth-death-rebirth.

The poem, an elegy, is thought to be based on an intensely personal experience of the poet. Just what that experience was is a favorite but fruitless field of speculation for Whitman's biographers. The poem asserts the triumph of the eternal life over death. The meaning of the poem is not stated explicitly, but it springs naturally from a recollection of the narrator's childhood days. Whitman imaginatively recreates the childhood experience of this inquiring lad and also shows how the boy becomes a man, and the man, a poet. This time sequence is as much the essence of the poem as is the growth of the consciousness of the poet. Memory plays an important part in this dramatic development. First, the boy tries to absorb the moving song of the mockingbird. Later, the boy replaces the bird as a significant character in the drama because he attempts to fuse the substance of the bird's song with the secret emanating from the sea; this synthesis is, in essence, his poetry. The word "death" is "delicious" because it is a prerequisite for rebirth. Thus the secret of life which the boy grasps from the sea is the recurrent pattern of birth-death-rebirth.

"Out of the Cradle Endlessly Rocking" is one of Whitman's great poems because of his use of image and symbol. The title itself is a symbol of birth. The sun and the moon, the land and the sea, and the stars and the sea waves contribute to the atmosphere and symbolic scenery in the poem. These images deepen the effect of the emotions in the poem, as in the bird's song, and are part of the dramatic structure. The poem is very melodious and rhythmic and may itself be compared to an aria (in opera, an aria is an elaborate melody sung by one voice). Its use of dactylic (/˘˘) and trochaic (/˘) meter is very appropriate in describing the motion of the sea waves and their meaning.

"When I Heard the Learn'd Astronomer"

The scholarly astronomer lectured with the aid of figures, charts, diagrams, and tables. Soon the poet felt tired and so he escaped from the lecture room and went outside, where he breathed "the mystical moist night-air" and "look'd up in perfect silence at the stars."

Whitman is saying that the true way to understand nature is not scientific but intuitive and mystical. The poet can feel and understand the processes of nature when he is experiencing them, but listening to people lecture about them merely makes him "tired and sick."

"Beat! Beat! Drums!"

Drumbeats and bugles resound through the buildings. The sounds "scatter the congregation" and disturb the bridegroom, the farmer, the city traffic, the sleepers, the talkers, the singers, and the lawyers. All these people hear the war cry, but the timid, the old, the children, and the mothers do not react positively to the call. The poet exhorts the drums and bugles to drown their dissenting voices. The drumbeat is a symbol of war and it creates highly passionate, even extremist responses; Whitman's poems reflect these emotions. The verse is characterized by a rapidity of movement which reflects the poet's enthusiasm, ardor, and passion. The poem also suggests Whitman's faith not only in the continuous cycle of history but also in the process of mystic evolution in the universe—that is, that the world will continue to progress in all spheres of life.

The poet expresses the spontaneous reaction of the North in the early years of the Civil War, following the South's attack on Fort Sumter in 1861. The three stanzas show the steady development of the theme. The poet feels the cause of war was justified by the events of that period. The drums, he says, should be able even "to shake the dead."

"Cavalry Crossing a Ford"

The poet describes the cavalry unit, "a line in long array," winding its "serpentine course" between two "green islands," the men's weapons shining in the sun. The soldiers become visible as they emerge from the "silvery river." These "brown-faced men" appear clearly, "each person a picture."

This is an excellent pictorial poem and Whitman presents two pictures in seven lines. The first picture is that of a cavalry unit winding its way to the river. The second picture, of the men entering and emerging from the river, has elements of individuation and distinctness in it. The poet renders a total picture by combining these elements and by giving them a graphic quality. Whitman is adept in handling movement and color, and both these elements contribute to the effect of the poem. The tone and the temper of the poem are also important. The poet's response to war here is less romantic than in the earlier poems of the group. The poet is face-to-face with the reality of war on the battlefront now.

"When Lilacs Last in the Dooryard Bloom'd"

"When Lilacs Last in the Dooryard Bloom'd" is an elegy on the death of Abraham Lincoln, though it never mentions the president by name. Like most elegies, it develops from the personal (the death of Lincoln and the poet's grief) to the impersonal (the death of "all of you" and death itself); from an intense feeling of grief to the thought of reconciliation. The poem, which is one of the finest Whitman ever wrote, is a dramatization of this feeling of loss. This elegy is grander and more touching than Whitman's other two elegies on Lincoln's death, "O Captain! My Captain!" and "Hush'd Be the Camps To-day." The form is elegiac but also contains elements found in operatic music, such as the aria and recitative. The song of the hermit thrush, for example, is an "aria."

Abraham Lincoln was shot in Washington, D.C., by Booth on April 14, 1865, and died the following day. The body was sent by train from Washington to Springfield, Illinois. As it crossed the continent, it was saluted by the people of America. Whitman has not only men and women but even natural objects saluting the dead man.

The first cycle of the poem, comprising sections 1-4, presents the setting in clear perspective. As spring returns, the lilacs blossom, and the planet Venus "nearly dropp'd in the western sky," the poet mourns the loss "of him I love." He mourns the "powerful western fallen star" now covered by "black murk" in the "tearful night," and he is "powerless" and "helpless" because the cloud around him "will not free my soul." He observes a lilac bush, is deeply affected by its perfume, and believes that "every leaf [is] a miracle." He breaks off a small branch with "heart-shaped leaves." A shy, solitary thrush, like a secluded hermit, sings a song which is an expression of its inmost grief. It sings "death's outlet song of life."

This first section of the poem introduces the three principal symbols of the poem—the lilac, the star, and the bird. They are woven into a poetic and dramatic pattern. The meaning of Whitman's symbols is neither fixed nor constant. The star, Venus, is identified with Lincoln, generally, but it also represents the poet's grief for the dead. Lilacs, which are associated with ever-returning spring, are a symbol of resurrection, while its heart-shaped leaves symbolize love. The purple color of the lilac, indicating the passion of the Crucifixion, is highly suggestive of the violence of Lincoln's death. The bird is the symbol of reconciliation with death and its song is the soul's voice. "Death's outlet song of life" means that out of death will come renewed life. Death is described as a "dark mother" or a "strong deliveress," which suggests that it is a necessary process for rebirth. The emotional drama in the poem is built around this symbolic framework. The continual recurrence of the spring season symbolizes the cycle of life and death and rebirth. The words "ever-returning spring," which occur in line 3 and are repeated in line 4, emphasize the idea of rebirth and resurrection. The date of Lincoln's assassination coincided with Easter, the time of Christ's resurrection. These two elements provide the setting to the poem in time and space.

The second stanza of the poem describes the poet's intense grief for the dead. Each line begins with "O," an exclamation which is like the shape of a mouth open in woe.

The second cycle of the poem comprises sections 5-9. It describes the journey of the coffin through natural scenery and industrial cities, both representing facets of American life. The thrush's song in section 4 is a prelude to the journey of the coffin which will pass "over the breast of the spring" through cities, woods, wheat fields, and orchards. But "in the midst of life we are in death," as it says in the Book of Common Prayer, and now the cities are "draped in black" and the states, like "crape-veil'd women," mourn and salute the dead. Somber faces, solemn voices, and mournful dirges mark the journey across the American continent.

To the dead man, the poet offers "my sprig of lilac," his obituary tribute. The poet brings fresh blossoms not for Lincoln alone, but for all men. He chants a song "for you O sane and sacred death" and offers flowers to "the coffins all of you O death."

The poet now addresses the star shining in the western sky: "Now I know what you must have meant." Last month the star seemed as if it "had something to tell" the poet. Whitman imagines that the star was full of woe "as the night advanced" until it vanished "in the netherward black of the night." Whitman calls upon the bird to continue singing. Yet the poet momentarily lingers on, held by the evening star, "my departing comrade."

The symbols are retained throughout this section. The poet bestows, as a mark of affection, a sprig of lilac on the coffin. The association of death with an object of growing life is significant. The star confides in the poet—a heavenly body identifies itself with an earthly being. The star is identified with Lincoln, and the poet is still under the influence of his personal grief for the dead body of Lincoln, and not yet able to perceive the spiritual existence of Lincoln after death. The song of the hermit thrush finally makes the poet aware of the deathless and the spiritual existence of Lincoln.

In the third cycle of the poem, sections 10-13, the poet wonders how he shall sing "for the large sweet soul that has gone." How shall he compose his tribute for the "dead one there I loved"? With his poem he wishes to "perfume the grave of him I love." The pictures on the dead president's tomb, he says, should be of spring and sun and leaves, a river, hills, and the sky, the city dense with dwellings, and people at work – in short, "all the scenes of life." The "body and soul" of America will be in them, the beauties of Manhattan spires as well as the shores of the Ohio and the Missouri rivers – all "the varied and ample land." The "gray-brown bird" is singing "from the swamps" its "loud human song" of woe. The song has a liberating effect on the poet's soul, although the star still holds him, as does the "mastering odor" of the lilac.

In this cycle the description of natural objects and phenomena indicates the breadth of Lincoln's vision, and the "purple" dawn, "delicious" eve, and "welcome" night suggest the continuous, endless cycle of the day, which, in turn, symbolizes Lincoln's immortality.

Sections 14-16 comprise a restatement of the earlier themes and symbols of the poem in a perspective of immortality. The poet remembers that one day while he sat in the peaceful but "unconscious scenery of my land," a cloud with a "long black trail" appeared and enveloped everything. Suddenly he "knew death." He walked between "the knowledge of death" and "the thought of death." He fled to the bird, who sang "the carol of death." The song of the thrush follows this passage. It praises death, which it describes as "lovely," "soothing," and "delicate." The "fathomless universe" is adored "for life and joy" and "sweet love." Death is described as a "dark mother always gliding near with soft feet." To her, the bird sings a song of "fullest welcome." Death is a "strong deliveress" to whom "the body gratefully" nestles.

The thrush's song is the spiritual ally of the poet. As the bird sings, the poet sees a vision: "And I saw askant the armies." He sees "battle-corpses" and the "debris of all the slain soldiers." These dead soldiers are happy in their resting places, but their parents and relatives continue to suffer because they have lost them. The suffering is not of the dead, but of the living.

The coffin has now reached the end of its journey. It passes "the visions," the "song of the hermit bird," and the "tallying song" of the poet's soul. "Death's outlet song" is heard, "sinking and fainting," and yet bursting with joy. The joyful psalm fills the earth and heaven. As the coffin passes him, the poet salutes it, reminding himself that the lilac blooming in the dooryard will return each spring. The coffin has reached its resting place in "the fragrant pines and the cedars dusk and dim." The star, the bird, and the lilac join with the poet as he bids goodbye to Lincoln, his "comrade," "the dead I loved so well."

The poet's realization of immortality through the emotional conflict of personal loss is the principal theme of this great poem, which is a symbolistic dramatization of the poet's grief and his ultimate reconciliation with the truths of life and death.

"As Consequent, Etc."

The poet declares that he sings "songs of continued years" which, like rivers, flow toward the sea. Life's new currents will soon merge with the streams of death. These currents flowing from the poet's self will join "the mystic ocean." The poet collects "vasting" from "the sea of Time" while the shells murmur the music of eternity.

This poem contains many of the themes of Whitman's poetry — his treatment of time and the problems of life, death, and eternity. The flow of the rivulets aptly suggests the spontaneous growth and unpremeditated movement of many of the poems included under the title *Autumn Rivulets*.

"There Was a Child Went Forth"

A child went out each day and the first object he saw, he became. That object continued to remain part of him either for a short while or for many years. Such objects as lilacs, grass, morning glories, March-born lambs, streets, oceans, clouds, and the horizon's edge became part of him, as did his parents and all other men and women. "These became part of that child who went forth every day, and who now goes, and will always go forth every day."

This poem expresses the poet's identification of his consciousness with all objects and forms, and the list of things which he himself identifies with is large and comprehensive and is a good example of Whitman's catalogs. The continual process of becoming is at the heart of the poem. We become something or grow into something and this is the process of becoming, of change and development. The interpenetration of the child's consciousness and physical phenomena, as shown in this poem, is one of the essential elements of Whitman's thought.

"Passage to India"

Whitman was greatly impressed by three great engineering achievements: the opening of the Suez Canal (1869), the laying of the transatlantic undersea cable (1866), and the joining of the Union Pacific and Central Pacific railroads at Utah to produce the nation's first transcontinental railway (1869). These events resulted in improved communication and travel, thus making possible a shorter passage to India. But in Whitman's poem, the completion of the physical journey to India is only a prelude to the spiritual pathway to India, the East, and, ultimately, to God.

The poet, in section 1, celebrates his time, singing of "the great achievements of the present," and listing "our modern wonders": the opening of the Suez Canal, the building of the great American railroad, and the laying of the transatlantic cable. Yet these achievements of the present have grown out of the past, "the dark unfathom'd retrospect." If the present is great, the past is greater because, like a projectile, the present is "impell'd by the past."

Here Whitman presents the world of physical reality, an antecedent to the world of spiritual reality. The essential idea in emphasizing the three engineering marvels is to indicate man's progress in terms of space. The space-time relationship is at the heart of the matter. The present is significant, but it is only an extension of the past and, therefore, its glories can be traced to times before. Man has mastered space, but he must enrich his spiritual heritage by evoking his past. His achievement in space will remain inadequate unless it is matched, or even surpassed, by his achievement in time and his spiritual values.

In section 2, Whitman envisages a passage to India which is illuminated by "Asiatic" and "primitive" fables. The fables of Asia and Africa are "the far-darting beams of the spirit," and the poet sings of the "deep diving bibles and legends." The spanning of the earth by scientific and technological means is only part of the divine scheme to have "the races, neighbors." The poet, therefore, sings of "a worship new," a spiritual passage to India.

The poet here identifies time with space and merges them in the realm of the spirit. Modern miracles of science are all part of a divine plan, of "God's purpose from the first." Thus the poet sings of a new religion which will combine the scientific achievements of the present with the spiritual attainments of the past.

Man's achievements in communications are shown in the portrayal of "tableaus twain" in section 3. The first tableau, or picture, is the first passage through the Suez Canal "initiated, open'd" by a "procession of steamships." The second picture is the journey of the railway cars "winding along the Platte" River to a junction of the Union and Central Pacific railroads. These two engineering achievements have given concrete shape to the dreams of the "Genoese," Columbus, "centuries after thou art laid in thy grave." Columbus dreamed of "tying the Eastern to the Western sea"; his ideal has now been fulfilled.

The underlying significance of the two events which Whitman describes here is to show that man's material advancement is only a means to his spiritual progress. The poet seems to master the vastness of space through his visionary power. And his thoughts also span time: modern achievements are a realization of Columbus' dream of linking East with West. His discovery of America was only a first step toward finding a shorter passage to India.

Section 4 tells how "many a captain" struggled to reach India. History seems like an underground stream which now and again rises to the surface. Thus Whitman praises Vasco da Gama, who discovered the sea route to India, and who thus accomplished the "purpose vast," the "rondure [rounding] of the world."

This is a tribute to the courage and adventurous spirit of the West in seeking a passage to India. The poet has a vision of history "as a rivulet running," and this dominates his sense of space. History is conceived of as a progression of continuous events which are like a flowing stream. This stream joins the spiritual sea and the poet's vision endows historical happenings with spiritual meaning.

Section 5 presents the spectacle of this earth "swimming in space," endowed with incredible beauty and power. Since the days of Adam and Eve, Whitman says, man has asked the meaning of life: "Who shall soothe these feverish children?/...Who speak the secret of impassive earth?" After the scientists and explorers have achieved their goals, the poet, who is "the true son of God," will forge the links of spiritual union. "Trinitas divine" will be achieved through the visionary power of the poet; he will fuse "Nature and Man."

The earth has been spanned by the efforts of engineers and technicians, Whitman says, and now it is for the poet to bring about the unity of East and West in the realm of the spirit. In his general survey of history, Whitman seems to encompass all time. The poet is the "true son of God" because, in visualizing the union of man and nature, he responds to the divine call within him. He is thus a true explorer and a discoverer of spiritual India.

In section 6, the poet sings of the "marriage of continents." Europe, Asia, Africa, and America are dancing "as brides and bridegrooms hand in hand." The "soothing cradle of man" is India. The poet perceives India as an ancient land of history and legend, morals and religion, adventure and challenge. Brahma and Buddha, Alexander and Tamerlane, Marco Polo and other "traders, rulers, explorers" all shared in its history. "The Admiral himself" (Columbus) is the chief historian. The poet says the culmination of heroic efforts is deferred for a long time. But eventually their seeds will sprout and bloom into a plant that "fills the earth with use and beauty."

Here Whitman has explored the swift passage of time and has invoked the India of Buddha through the present achievement of the linkage of continents by modern technology. The poet thus becomes a time-binder. He also attempts to fuse the familiar with the unfamiliar and the physical with the spiritual. He stands "curious in time," but he also stands outside of time, in eternity, in his spiritual quest.

Section 7 confirms that a passage to India is indeed a journey of the soul "to primal thought." It is not confined to "lands and seas alone." It is a passage back to the Creation, to innocence, "to realms of budding bibles." Whitman is anxious for himself and his soul to begin their journey.

The language of section 7 is highly metaphorical. The return of the poet and his soul to the East is envisaged as a journey back to the cradle of mankind, to the East, where many religions had their birth. It is a journey "back to wisdom's birth, to innocent intuitions." The poet and his soul seek a mystical experience of union with God in the realm of the spirit.

In section 8, the poet and his soul are about to "launch out on trackless seas" and to sail "on waves of ecstasy" singing "our song of God." The soul pleases the poet, and the poet pleases the soul, and they begin their spiritual exploration. They believe in God "but with the mystery of God we dare not dally." They think "silent thoughts, of Time and Space and Death." The poet addresses God as "O Thou transcendent,/Nameless," as the source of light and cosmic design and a "moral, spiritual fountain." Whitman "shrivels at the thought of God,/At Nature and its wonders," but he expects the soul to bring about a harmonious reconciliation with these forces. When the soul accomplishes its journey and confronts God, it will be as if it had found an older brother. It will finally melt "in fondness in his arms."

The last two sections of this poem are marked by an upsurge of spiritual thought and an ecstatic experience. The poet and his soul, like two lovers, are united in harmony. They seek the mystical experience of union with God. The poet reflects on the nature of God as a transcendental deity. By comprehending God, the poet is enabled to comprehend himself and also man's complex relationship with time, space, and death. The soul is eternal and establishes its relationship with time. The soul is vast and expansive and thus forms a relationship with space. The soul is alive forever and thus conquers death.

In section 8, the poet and his soul together seek to perceive the Divine Reality. Both eagerly await a mystical experience of union with God, of merging with the Divine Being. God is conceived of as a "fountain" or "reservoir" and this image is similar to the basic metaphor of water, which is necessary to nourish the "greenery" of *Leaves of Grass*.

In section 9, the journey which the soul embarks on is a "passage to more than India." It is a challenging spiritual journey. Whitman asks the soul if it is ready: "Are thy wings plumed indeed for such far flights?" The passage to the divine shores, to the "aged fierce enigmas," and to the "strangling problems" is filled with difficulty and "skeletons, that, living, never reach'd you"—but it is a thrilling journey. The poet, fired by the spirit of Columbus, is intent on seeking an "immediate passage" because "the blood burns in my veins." He "will risk... all" in this bold and thrilling adventure; but actually it is safe enough, for "are they not all the seas of God"? Thus the passage to India—and more—is a journey of man through the seas of God in search of an ideal. It is marked by intense spiritual passion.

This last section presents the final evolution of the symbol of India, which began as a geographical entity and culminated in a timeless craving of man for the realization of God. The words "passage" and "India" both have an evolving symbolic meaning and significance in this richly evocative poem and the growth of their meanings is indirectly the growth of the poem itself.

"The Sleepers"

This poem had no title in the 1855 edition, and was called "Night Poem" in 1856 and "Sleep-Chasings" in 1860. It was entitled "The Sleepers" in 1871. The changes in the title indicate a progressive change of direction in the meaning of the poem. The dominant symbolism of the poem is implied in the earlier title "Night Poem." Night is a rather common symbol for death; sleep implies death and, at the same time, the release of the soul through death. "Sleep-Chasings" indicate the technique of the poem. The poet identifies himself as merging with other beings and multitudes of beings and thus establishes a spiritual and psychological kinship with them. At first the images and the structure seem to be disorganized, but they have an underlying unity which emerges out of the stream-of-consciousness technique. The symbolism is not quite clear in the earlier sections but becomes more meaningful and explicit in the last two sections, especially in the last ten lines of the poem.

Structurally, this poem appears to be a technical innovation, though the theme seems elusive at first and the structure rather loose. The poet's vision or dream motif is the core of the structure and the apparent lack of organization reflects the quality of the dream itself. Thus the poem's structure, theme, and symbolism are brought into a cohesive and meaningful pattern. The last ten lines are marked by a religious tone and express the idea of reincarnation. The poem grows from a condition of sleep and of sleepers to a state of awakening and of wakers, from the time of night to the time of day. The structure of the poem shows the growth of the poet's consciousness and experience of the inner life.

In section 1, the poet wanders all night "in my vision" and observes the human scene. His state is "confused." He sees all the people sleeping: "the little children in their cradles," the "white features of corpses," the "livid faces of drunkards," the "new-born emerging from gates, and the dying emerging from gates." Later the poet observes loving sleepers: "the married couple," "the sisters," and the mother with her little child. The blind, the deaf, the prisoners, the unrequited lovers—all are sleeping. The earth seems to recede from the poet as he stands near "the worst-suffering." Then the poet imagines himself in different roles. He becomes other sleepers, and he dreams their dreams. The poet thus gives himself up to the mysteries of the night and the unreal world of dreams. He recounts some of those dreams.

The progression of the first section is akin to the semi-rational, semi-erratic quality of consciousness. The section concerns the poet's identification with various characters who are sleepers in different states of slumber. It is the range and quality of the human scene which is significant. Life is observed from the condition of birth to that of death. Simultaneously, the emotions which affect the sleepers subconsciously become the objects of the poet's identification. The poet becomes one with the night and darkness. Thus he pierces the darkness and observes the beauty of the eternal. This is the poet's mystical vision which penetrates the world of matter and reaches the reality of the spirit. The matter-of-fact world ends and the unreal world of dreams begins. The joy of the merging is similar to the ecstasy of sexual fulfillment. The imagery is vividly physical and sexual and was criticized on that account; consequently, for later editions, the poet modified the text. But the idea of the poet's merging with the night being comparable to the joy of sexual experience remains clear and compelling.

In section 2, the poet, still identifying himself with other dreamers, first assumes the role of an old woman: "It is my face yellow and wrinkled instead of the old woman's." Later he sees a shroud and he becomes a shroud. In the coffin, "it is not evil or pain here, it is blank here." Thus, says the poet, "everything in the light and air ought to be happy/...he has enough."

This section shows more identification of the poet—this time, with objects. He enters a coffin to experience death, and this experience, by contrast, makes him aware of the value of life. All the poet's experiences are facets of his total vision of life.

The poet, in section 3, sees a "beautiful gigantic swimmer" and observes "his white body" and "undaunted eyes." He implores the waves not to kill "the courageous giant...in the prime of his middle age." The swimmer struggles hard but is defeated by "the slapping eddies." The corpse swiftly passes out of the poet's sight.

The disorganized dream sequence has now ended, and sections 3 and 4 are both clearly and coherently formed. The images in both sections are drawn from death by the sea and are very meaningfully expressed. In section 3, the poet observes a swimmer. The seashore is a symbol of the gulf that separates life from death. The handsome swimmer is pitted against the sea in an unequal struggle; the triumph of the ocean against man is a recurrent theme in American literature. Man is defeated by the sea; but the sea is also a symbol of the world of the spirit. Thus spiritual reality is realized by man through death.

The poet is deeply involved, in section 4, and therefore unable to "extricate" himself from the experience of death on the seashore. The "razory ice-wind" causes a shipwreck. The poet hears "the burst as she strikes." He rushes to the surf but is unable to help. All he can do is wait until the next morning to "help pick up the dead and lay them in rows in a barn."

As man is the principal object of section 3, the ship is the central image of section 4. The death of the swimmer is paralleled by the wreck of the ship; these two scenes of destruction are the two aspects of the poet's experience of death by the sea. The description and imagery of the shipwreck are effectively presented.

Section 5 recounts a scene of General Washington in Brooklyn "amid a crowd of officers," unable to express his grief over the killing. With the coming of peace, Washington bids good-bye to his soldiers. He stands in a room and the "speechless" officers give him a loving farewell.

Here Whitman is again using the technique of a backward and forward movement in time and space. In this section, a backward movement is conceived in terms of time as the poet recalls General Washington. The poet's vision triumphs over time and space. In evoking the memory of the Founding Fathers, he establishes a link with the past.

Whitman recollects, in section 6, an experience of his mother's "when she was a nearly grown girl" and lived with her parents. An Indian woman visited their homestead in the morning and stayed until mid-afternoon. The "red squaw" was a person of "wonderful beauty and purity" and the poet's mother was delighted by her. She thought of her and watched for her for a long time, but the Indian woman never returned.

This is yet another scene of spiritual love. The bond that united Washington with his soldiers (section 5) was personal and spiritual. The description of the spiritual affinity between the poet's mother and the Indian woman is delicately drawn. It gives all the significant details, is realistic, down-to-earth, and precise. She is an embodiment of primeval purity and beauty. The impression she makes is so deep that the poet's mother thinks of her for a long time afterward. This longing and fondness is similar to a romantic quest.

Sections 5 and 6, the scenes of Washington and of the Indian woman, present a contrast to the scenes of shipwreck and death in sections 3 and 4. Scenes of separation and frustration are followed by those of union and fulfillment.

In section 7, the poet's mood changes again. He has been in "contact of something unseen—an amour of the light and air." The seasons become part of him and his dreams. "Elements merge in the night," people recall their pasts in dreams and imagine themselves to be living in the past again. "The Dutchman voyages home, and the Scotchman...voyages home.../To every port of England, France, Spain, enter well-fill'd ships." These "immigrants," like "the beautiful lost swimmer," "the red squaw," and all other people are restored to health by sleep—and made equal to each other, too: "one is no better than the other." They are all beautiful. The universe is orderly and everything is in its proper place. They are all different but are united in sleep. "The diverse shall be no less diverse, but they shall flow and unite—they unite now."

A notable image of this section is that of light. The poet experiences "an amour of the light and air." The imagery of light suggests the illumination resulting from Whitman's mystical experience. This section also exemplifies Whitman's technique of presenting a series of men and objects in quick progression, illustrative of diversity, but also an initial step to the idea of unity.

Other images are those of return and of beauty. The imagery of men returning to their original homes perhaps suggests the return of the world to its origins, of man to his primeval abode, in a process of spiritual renewal.

Men and women become beautiful in sleep. Beauty, associated with darkness, attains a spiritual quality which is the essential element in the poet's mystical experience here. The beautiful sleepers "flow hand in hand over the whole earth" in section 8. All are linked together in harmony. They become beautiful in the "invigoration" and the "chemistry" of the night. Hearts flow freely into hearts, and barriers are broken. This is the miraculous effect of the night. The poet, too, surrenders himself to the charm of the night. Although he loves "the rich running day," he does not ignore the night. He desires ultimately to return to his "mother," the night.

The poet here hints at the concept of reincarnation. He passes from the night, but he returns to her again. The night is a vast reservoir of spiritual energy, and the poet, on shedding his earthly garments, wishes to join his mother, the vast realm of the spirit, to find fulfillment of his own self.

"To a Locomotive in Winter"

The locomotive is hailed as the object of the poet's declamatory song: "Thee for my recitative." Its "black cylindric body" with the "head-light fix'd in front" contains its "fierce-throated beauty." It is presented as the epitome "of the modern." It is an "emblem of motion and power," and the poet calls upon it to "serve the Muse" and "roll through my chant."

The locomotive is presented as a symbol of the impressive technological progress of America in the 1870s. Whitman fits it into his own system of values and his concept of poetry. He believed that technological objects were fitting subjects for poetry. Here, many technical appearances of the locomotive – for example, side-bars and connecting rods – are described. He asks the locomotive to "merge in verse," which indicates his attitude to the issue of science and poetry; Whitman does not think there is any real conflict between them. The term "recitative" used in relation to the locomotive suggests its musical and operatic effects: the engine's roar is music. The locomotive also becomes a symbol of the spirit and has its own place in the harmonious scheme of the universe.

"As the Time Draws Nigh"

As the time of death draws near, the poet is affected by "a dread beyond of/I know not what" that casts a gloom on his spirits. He will "traverse the States," but perhaps his "singing voice" may "suddenly cease." He asks: "O chants! must all then amount to but this?" But in this awareness of his approaching end, he is reassured by the fact that he and his soul have at least "positively appear'd."

Two divergent moods are expressed in this poem. In a mood of despair, the poet wonders why the journey of life should end. But then he discovers that death is also a new beginning, a new life. Then, the fear of departure is combined with the hope of a new arrival. This emotional and philosophical paradox is at the heart of the poem. A touch of deeply felt personal emotion marks expressions such as "a dread beyond of/I know not what darkens me." This is reminiscent of the lines in Hamlet's famous soliloquy, "the dread of something after death–/The undiscover'd country" (*Hamlet* III, i, 78-79).

"So Long!"

The poet remembers his promise that as his "leaves" blossomed, he would raise his joyous voice at the "consummations" of his ideals and objectives. When "America does what was promis'd"–that is, fulfills her promise–he will have a sense of fulfillment. In reviewing his work, he takes note of his announcements on justice, liberty, equality, the identity of the states and the Union, adhesiveness, the great individual, the copious life, the "race of splendid...men." The best of him, he says, will remain embodied in these announcements. In a passionate tone he asks: "Is there a single final farewell?" His songs "cease"; he "abandons" them and advances "solely" toward the reader. *Leaves of Grass* is himself: "Camerado, this is no book,/ Who touches this touches a man." In a final note of farewell, Whitman addresses his reader: "I love you, I depart from materials,/I am as one disembodied, triumphant, dead."

This poem has a double meaning. It is an expression of both a welcome and a farewell. Whitman reviews his message, anticipates life in death, and looks forward to the "athletic bands" which will be created and inspired by his *Leaves*. The poet, who has a prophetic tone of voice, creates the illusion of his physical person in words such as "this is no book...[but] a man." The concluding note is mystical because the poet looks to "an unknown sphere," moves away from "materials," and ceases to be merely physical. Thus the journey of his life ends at a destination which is the fulfillment of the mystical urge.

"Queries to My Seventieth Year"

The poet, approaching his seventieth year, wonders whether the "uncertain spectre" of the future will bring him life or death. Will it bring strength or weakness, activity or paralysis? Will it "stir the waters" even yet? Will it leave him "dull...and old"? Or will it happily cut off his journey?

This is an almost autobiographical composition. The poet wonders whether his pursuit of the life of the spirit will continue or whether it will end abruptly. The uncertainty involved in the autumn of life is effectively presented.

"America"

The poet thinks of America as the "centre of equal daughters, equal sons," who are "strong, ample, fair, enduring, capable," and who identify themselves with "Freedom, Law and Love." He salutes America as the "grand, sane, towering, seated Mother," who is "chair'd in the adamant of Time."

This short poem is a reassertion of the poet's faith in the destiny of the American nation. It demonstrates his love of the masses, his devotion to democracy, and his belief that in responding to the call of a democratic process, America is fulfilling a spiritual need of her people.

"Good-Bye My Fancy!"

The poet bids a sad farewell to his fancy, his imagination: "Farewell dear mate, dear love!" He doesn't know where he will go or whether he will ever encounter his fancy again. For a long time, the poet and his fancy "lived, joy'd, caress'd together," and now comes the moment of their separation. Yet there are no regrets because the poet has become almost one with his fancy. He even hopes to be united with her again. Maybe in leaving him, fancy is really ushering him "to the true songs," and therefore he declares: "Good-bye—and hail! my Fancy."

This is the final poem of *Leaves of Grass* proper. The central core of the poem is Whitman's identification with his fancy; and what is identified is the poet's body, not his soul. The "I" in this poem is the body, and the farewell is prompted by the body's impending dissolution. The tone of the poem is surely plaintive, but the poet's pessimism is not very deep. Whitman slowly and steadily realizes the true importance of his association with his fancy. The union between body and fancy paves the way for the transformation of the physical world, since fancy has the power to enable the poet to visualize the world of bliss.

Despite the serious nature of the theme, Whitman has maintained an informal, intimate tone and atmosphere in the poem. The diction is colloquial—for instance, "let me look back a moment" and "may-be we'll be better off." Finally, this poem expresses Whitman's belief that fancy will conquer death and be a harbinger of immortality.

CRITICAL ANALYSIS

FORM

Leaves of Grass belongs to no particular accepted form of poetry. Whitman described its form as "a new and national declamatory expression." Whitman was a poet bubbling with energy and burdened with sensations, and his poetic utterances reveal his innovations. His poetry seems to grow organically, like a tree. It has the tremendous vitality of an oak. Its growth follows no regular pattern: "Song of Myself," for example, seems at first almost recklessly written, without any attention to form. Whitman's poetry, like that of most prophetic writers, is unplanned, disorganized, sometimes abortive, but nevertheless distinctively his own.

STYLE

Musical Elements

Whitman believed that poetry should be spoken, not written, and this basic criterion governed the concept and form of his poetry. He used repetition and reiterative devices (as, for example, in "Out of the Cradle Endlessly Rocking," the lines "Loud! loud! loud!" and "Blow! blow! blow!") He also employed elements of the opera (the aria and the recitative) in his poems.

Language

Whitman was a master of exuberant phrases and images: "The beautiful uncut hair of graves" ("Song of Myself," section 6) is extraordinarily descriptive. Conversely, another description of the grass in the same section of the same poem, where it is described as "the handkerchief of the Lord," is trivial.

Whitman brought vitality and picturesqueness to his descriptions of the physical world. He was particularly sensitive to sounds and described them with acute awareness. His view of the world was dominated by its change and fluidity, and this accounts for his frequent use of "ing" forms, either present participle or gerund.

Whitman's language is full of his eccentricities: he used the word "presidentiad" for presidency, "pave" for pavement, and he spelled Canada with a *K*.

Leaves of Grass contains archaic expressions—for example, betimes, betwixt, methinks, haply, and list (for listen). Whitman also employs many colloquial expressions and technical and commercial terms. Words from foreign languages add color and variety to his style.

Rhythm and Meter

Whitman's use of rhythms is notable. A line of his verse, if scanned in the routine way, seems like a prose sentence, or an advancing wave of prose rhythm. Yet his work is composed in lines, not in sentences as prose would be. The line is the unit of sense in Whitman.

Whitman experimented with meter, rhythm, and form because he thought that experimentation was the law of the changing times, and that innovation was the gospel of the modern world.

Whitman's fondness for trochaic movement rather than iambic movement shows the distinctive quality of his use of meter. An iamb is a metrical foot of two syllables, the second of which is accented (∪/). A trochee is a metrical foot consisting of an accented syllable followed by an unaccepted one (/∪). The iambic is the most commonly used meter in English poetry, partly because of the structure of English speech. English phrases normally begin with an article, preposition, or conjunction which merges into the word that follows it, thus creating the rising inflection which is iambic. Why, then, did Whitman prefer the trochaic to the iambic meter? It was partly due to the poet's desire for declamatory expression and oratorical style, since the trochee is more suitable for eloquent expression than the iambic meter. Whitman also liked to do things that were unusual and novel.

Imagery

Imagery means a figurative use of language. Whitman's use of imagery shows his imaginative power, the depth of his sensory perceptions, and his capacity to capture reality instantaneously. He expresses his impressions of the world in language which mirrors the present. He makes the past come alive in his images and makes the future seem immediate. Whitman's imagery has some logical order on the conscious level, but it also delves into the subconscious, into the world of memories, producing a stream-of-consciousness of images. These images seem like parts of a dream, pictures of fragments of a world. On the other hand, they have solidity; they build the structure of the poems.

Symbolism

A symbol is an emblem, a concrete object that stands for something abstract; for example, the dove is a symbol of peace;

the cross, Christianity. Literary symbols, however, have a more particular connotation. They sometimes signify the total meaning, or the different levels of meaning, which emerge from the work of art in which they appear. A white whale is just an animal —but in Melville's *Moby Dick* it is a god to some characters, evil incarnate to others, and a mystery to others. In other words, it has an extended connotation which is symbolic.

In the mid-1880s, the Symbolist movement began in France, and the conscious use of symbols became the favorite practice of poets. The symbolists and Whitman had much in common; both tried to interpret the universe through sensory perceptions, and both broke away from traditional forms and methods. But the symbols of the French symbolists were highly personal, whereas in Whitman the use of the symbol was governed by the objects he observed: the sea, the birds, the lilacs, the calamus plant, the sky, and so on. Nevertheless, Whitman did have an affinity with the symbolists; they even translated some of his poems into French.

THEMES

Whitman's major concern was to explore, discuss, and celebrate his own self, his individuality and his personality. Second, he wanted to eulogize democracy and the American nation with its achievements and potential. Third, he wanted to give poetical expression to his thoughts on life's great, enduring mysteries—birth, death, rebirth or resurrection, and reincarnation.

The Self

To Whitman, the complete self is both physical and spiritual. The self is man's individual identity, his distinct quality and being, which is different from the selves of other men, although it can identify with them. The self is a portion of the one Divine Soul. Whitman's critics have sometimes confused the concept of self with egotism, but this is not valid. Whitman is constantly talking about "I," but the "I" is universal, a part of the Divine, and therefore not egotistic.

The Body and the Soul

Whitman is a poet of both these elements in man, the body and the soul. He thought that we could comprehend the soul only through the medium of the body. To Whitman, all matter is as divine as the soul; since the body is as sacred and as spiritual as the soul, when he sings of the body or its performances, he is singing a spiritual chant.

Nature

Whitman shares the Romantic poet's relationship with nature. To him, as to Emerson, nature is divine and an emblem of God. The universe is not dead matter, but full of life and meaning. He loves the earth, the flora and fauna of the earth, the moon and stars, the sea, and all other elements of nature. He believes that man is nature's child and that man and nature must never be disjoined.

Time

Whitman's concept of the ideal poet is, in a way, related to his ideas on time. He conceives of the poet as a time-binder, one who realizes that the past, present, and future are "not disjoined, but joined," that they are all stages in a continuous flow and cannot be considered as separate and distinct. These modern ideas of time have given rise to new techniques of literary expression —for example, the stream-of-consciousness viewpoint.

Cosmic Consciousness

Whitman believed that the cosmos, or the universe, does not consist merely of lifeless matter; it has awareness. It is full of life and filled with the spirit of God. The cosmos is God and God is the cosmos; death and decay are unreal. This cosmic consciousness is, indeed, one aspect of Whitman's mysticism.

Mysticism

Mysticism is an experience that has a spiritual meaning which is not apparent to the senses nor to the intellect. Thus mysticism, an insight into the real nature of man, God, and the universe, is attained through one's intuition. The mystic believes in the unity of God and man, man and nature, God and the universe. To a mystic, time and space are unreal, since both can be overcome by man by spiritual conquest. Evil, too, is unreal, since God is present everywhere. Man communicates with his soul in a mystical experience, and Whitman amply expresses his responses to the soul in *Leaves of Grass*, especially in "Song of Myself." He also expresses his mystical experience of his body or personality being permeated by the supernatural. Whitman's poetry is his artistic expression of various aspects of his mystical experience.

Death

Whitman deals with death as a fact of life. Death in life is a fact, but life in death is a truth for Whitman; he is thus a poet of matter and of spirit.

Transcendentalism

Transcendentalism, which originated with German philosophers, became a powerful movement in New England between 1815 and 1836. Emerson's *Nature* (1836) was a manifesto of American transcendental thought. It implied that the true reality is the spirit and that it lies beyond the reach or realm of the senses. The area of sensory perceptions must be transcended to reach the spiritual reality. American transcendentalism accepted the findings of contemporary science as materialistic counterparts of spiritual achievement. Whitman's "Passage to India" demonstrates this approach. The romanticist in Whitman is combined with the transcendentalist in him. His quest for transcendental truths is highly individualistic and therefore his thought, like Emerson's, is often unsystematic and prophetic.

Personalism

Whitman used the term "personalism" to indicate the fusion of the individual with the community in an ideal democracy. He believed that every man at the time of his birth receives an identity, and this identity is his "soul." The soul, finding its abode in man, is individualized, and man begins to develop his personality. The main idea of personalism is that the person is the be-all of all things; it is the source of consciousness and the senses. One *is* because *God* is; therefore, man and God are one—one personality. Man's personality craves immortality because it desires to follow the personality of God. This idea is in accord with Whitman's notion of the self. Man should first become himself, which is also the way of coming closer to God. Man should comprehend the divine soul within him and realize his identity and the true relationship between himself and God. This is the doctrine of personalism.

Democracy

Whitman had a deep faith in democracy because this political form of government respects the individual. He thought that the genius of the United States is best expressed in the common people, not in its executive branch or legislature, or in its churches or law courts. He believed that it is the common folk who have a deathless attachment to freedom. His attitudes can be traced to the Enlightenment of the eighteenth century because he thought that the source of evil lay in oppressive social institutions rather than in human nature. The function of literature is to break away from the feudal past of man and artistically to urge the democratic present. Princes and nobles hold no charm for Whitman; he sings of the average, common man. He follows Emerson in applauding the doctrine of the "divine average" and of the greatness of the commonplace. A leaf of grass, to Whitman, is as important as the heavenly motion of the stars. Whitman loves America, its panoramic scenery and its processional view of diverse, democratically inclined people. He loved, and reveled in, the United States as a physical entity, but he also visualized it as a New World of the spirit. Whitman is a singer of the self as well as a trumpeter of democracy because he believes that only in a free society can individuals attain self-hood.

Whitman emphasized individual virtue, which he believed would give rise to civic virtue. He aimed at improving the masses by first improving the individual, thus becoming a true spiritual democrat. His idea of social and political democracy—that all men are equal before the law and have equal rights—is harmonized with his concept of spiritual democracy—that people have immense possibilities and a measureless wealth of latent power for spiritual attainment. In fact, he bore with the failings of political democracy primarily because he had faith in spiritual democracy, in creating and cultivating individuals who, through comradeship, would contribute to the ideal society. This view of man and society is part of Whitman's poetic program.

THE QUINTESSENTIAL AMERICAN POET

In 1920, Van Wyck Brooks wrote that Whitman was the "focal center" of American creative experience and literary expression. The poet combined within him elements of native realism and of New England philosophy which made him a truly national spiritual synthesis. But modern criticism does not view Whitman as the quintessential American poet, or the national norm; other writers, such as Emerson, Thoreau, Melville, and Hawthorne may be equally regarded as national norms. Whitman, no doubt, embodied many qualities of the American character—for example, its variousness, diversity, adventurousness, and pioneering spirit—yet he was not the only national norm. To us today, submerged as we are in specialization, Whitman has a particular appeal because he symbolizes variety, largeness, and the tendency toward innovation.

WHITMAN'S ACHIEVEMENT

Walt Whitman's achievement as a poet and prophet is truly monumental. He exercised a deep influence on his immediate successors in American letters, and even on modern poets, although he himself was a highly individualistic poet. As a symbolist, his influence was felt in Europe, where he was considered the greatest poet America had yet produced. His high style and elevated expression found echoes in Emily Dickinson, Hart Crane, Marianne Moore, and others. Whitman as a stylist is the culmination of the sublime tradition in America, and even Allen Ginsberg, so different from Whitman in so many respects, follows the Whitman tradition of using invocative language. Whitman, though a man of his age, an essentially nineteenth-century poet, exercised a profound influence on twentieth-century poets and modern poetry in the use of language, in the processes of symbol and image-making, in exercising great freedom in meter and form, and in cultivating the individualistic mode. In many ways Whitman is modern because he is prophetic; he is a poet not only of America but of the whole of mankind. He has achieved the Olympian stature and the rare distinction of a world poet.

SELECTED BIBLIOGRAPHY

ALLEN, GAY WILSON. *The Solitary Singer.* New York: Macmillan, 1955.

______. "On the Trochaic Meter of 'Pioneers! O Pioneers!'" *American Literature,* XX (1949): 449-51.

______. *Walt Whitman Handbook.* Chicago: Packward and Company, 1946.

______. *Walt Whitman as Man, Poet, and Legend.* Carbondale: Southern Illinois University Press, 1955.

______. "Whitman's 'When Lilacs Last in the Dooryard Bloom'd,'" *The Explicator,* X (1952): 55.

ASSELINEAU, ROGER. *The Evolution of Walt Whitman: The Development of a Personality.* Cambridge: Harvard University Press, 1960.

BLODGETT, HAROLD. *The Best of Whitman.* New York: Ronald Press, 1953.

BLODGETT, HAROLD, and BRADLEY, SCULLEY, ed. *Leaves of Grass, Comprehensive Reader's Edition.* New York: New York University Press, 1965.

BOWERS, FREDSON. *Textual and Literary Criticism.* Cambridge, England: Cambridge University Press, 1959.

BRADLEY, SCULLEY, ed. *Leaves of Grass and Selected Prose.* New York: Holt, Rinehart and Winston, 1949.

BRIGGS, ARTHUR E. *Walt Whitman, Thinker and Artist.* New York: Philosophical Library, 1952.

CARGIL, OSCAR. *Leaves of Grass.* New York: Harper, 1950.

CHARI, V. K. *Whitman in the Light of Vedantic Mysticism.* Lincoln: Nebraska University Press, 1964.

CHASE, RICHARD. *Walt Whitman Reconsidered.* New York: Sloane, 1955.

COFFMAN, S. K. "'Crossing Brooklyn Ferry,' a Note on the Catalog Technique in Whitman's Poetry," *Modern Philology,* LI (1954): 225-32.

COOKE, ALICE LOVELACE. "A Note on Whitman's Symbolism in 'Song of Myself,'" *Modern Language Notes,* LXV (1950): 228-32.

COWLEY, MALCOLM. *Leaves of Grass: The First Edition.* New York: Viking, 1959.

DAVIS, C. T., and ALLEN, G. W. *Walt Whitman's Poems, Selections with Critical Aids.* New York: New York University Press, 1955.

DE SELINCOURT, ERNEST. *Walt Whitman: A Critical Study.* New York: Russell and Russell, 1965.

GEISMAR, MAXWELL. *The Walt Whitman Reader.* New York: Pocket Books, Inc., 1955.

HOLLOWAY, EMORY. *Free and Lonesome Heart: The Secret of Walt Whitman.* New York: Vintage Press, 1960.

——. *Leaves of Grass: The Collected Poems of Walt Whitman.* New York: The Book League of America, 1942.

LAWRENCE, D. H. *Studies in Classic American Literature.* New York: Viking, 1964 (originally published in 1923).

LOVELL, JOHN, JR. "Appreciating Whitman: 'Passage to India,'" *Modern Language Quarterly,* XXI (1960): 131-41.

MILLER, JAMES E. *A Critical Guide to Leaves of Grass.* Chicago: University of Chicago Press, 1957.

——. *Walt Whitman.* New York: Twayne, 1962.

——, ed. *Whitman's "Song of Myself": Origin, Growth, and Meaning.* New York: Dodd, Mead, 1964.

MUSGROVE, S. *T. S. Eliot and Walt Whitman.* Wellington: New Zealand University Press, 1952.

PEARCE, ROY HARVEY. *Whitman: Twentieth Century Views.* New Jersey: Prentice Hall, 1962.

TRAUBEL, HORACE. *With Walt Whitman in Camden.* Carbondale: Southern Illinois University Press, 1959.

VAN DOREN, MARK. "Walt Whitman the Poet," *Walt Whitman: Man, Poet and Philosopher, Three Lectures.* Washington, Library of Congress, 1955.

NOTES

NOTES

NOTES